Green Card Brides

ALSO BY YASIN KAKANDE

The Ambitious Struggle
(2013)

Slave States
(2015)

Why We Are Coming
(2020)

A Murder of Hate
(2025)

Green Card Brides

The Lives of Black Migrants in America

Yasin Kakande

BLACK WRITERS INK LLC
Boxborough, MA, 2024

BLACK WRITERS INK LLC
318 Codman Hill Road
Boxborough, Massachusetts

www.blackwritersink.com

First Edition 2024
Copyright ©2024 by Yasin Kakande
All rights reserved

Book design: Pablo Capra

ISBN
Paperback 979-8-9909844-0-0
Ebook 979-8-9909844-1-7

Printed in the United States of America

Contents

Dedication

To the memory of my mother,
Hajjati Hadija Nakkazi.

Declaration

The events and experiences in this book are based on true stories, but certain names and details have been altered to ensure the confidentiality and anonymity of the people involved.

Introduction

A WEEK after my arrival in the United States, I visited with an old school friend, Musa from Uganda. We were driving north on I-95 from Boston when he nearly missed our exit and switched lanes rapidly. A police car suddenly appeared behind us, blue lights flashing.

Musa pulled over to the side of the road. When we'd been waiting for a few minutes, I nudged him. "Why aren't you getting out of the car?" I asked, because in Uganda you're expected to step out of your car and talk with the police if they stop you.

Musa stared at me like I'd lost my mind. "Here in the U.S., don't *ever* get out of the car if you're stopped," he warned. "It's considered disrespectful.

Besides, we're Black men. The police might shoot us for being aggressive. You have to do whatever you can to prove you are harmless."

If I were ever driving and got stopped, he added, "You must stay calm and be polite. Don't take your wallet out of your pocket unless you tell the officer exactly what you're doing. If you move your hands too quickly, they can shoot you."

I'm an investigative journalist with an MBA, nearly forty years old, and the father of five children. I wasn't even the one driving the car. Yet, as the police officer approached, my back went rigid with fear and my forehead broke out in a sweat.

Not for the first time, I wondered if coming to the U.S. was a mistake.

I've been expelled from two Middle Eastern countries because of my reporting on migrant rights, and left Uganda after my reporting provoked threats on my life. I arrived in the U.S. in 2017, when refugees were fleeing their countries due to armed conflicts, poverty, and climate change, provoking an unprecedented refugee crisis as countries began locking down their borders against them.

That first stop by a police officer in the U.S. was five years ago. Since then, I have discovered firsthand exactly what it means to be a Black migrant worker in the United States—someone who has no choice but to take 3D (dirty, dangerous, and demeaning) jobs. I have been harassed, called ignorant and dirty, and told to go back to Africa even by Black Americans.

During the global Covid-19 pandemic, I have been a caregiver, an essential worker in nursing homes, juvenile institutions, and private residences. Yet, I am often treated as invisible and irrelevant, or as a terrifying threat, either because of the color of my skin, or because others see me as a thief stealing jobs from American workers.

More than once, I have asked myself what I'm doing here. I miss my family and country with an ache so acute that it's often physical.

*

The last time I saw my father, Edirisa Kalule, he was on his deathbed. Nearly skeletal, his face was contorted in pain, and his skin was pale and dry. His usual confident, booming voice scarcely rose above a whisper. Dust motes swirled in the sunlight above bags of rice stacked about the room for Ramadan. My father's existence on this earth, in that husk of a body, seemed scarcely more substantial than the dust.

After being deported by the government in Dubai for my investigative reporting, I had returned home to Uganda with the hope of carving out a life for myself and my family as a veteran journalist with advanced degrees. It was, as they say in the U.S., an epic fail. I was rapidly sinking into poverty and my life was being threatened.

Ugandan government officials and corporate executives were making threats against me, my wife, and children because I'd continued writing about the human rights abuses of Black migrant workers for news organizations like Reuters and Al Jazeera, and for Migrant-Rights (https://www.migrant-rights.org), a web site I helped found to raise awareness of the plight of migrant workers around the world, who work and live in hazardous conditions for low pay and with few legal rights. These threats began after I published a series of freelance articles investigating an agreement a Ugandan recruiting company made to send college graduates to Saudi Arabia and Dubai to fill jobs. Once the Ugandans arrived, they were essentially trapped, subjected to hazardous working conditions for low pay, with very little legal recourse for escaping what essentially amounted to slave labor.

Needless to say, the recruiting company, which had connections to top Ugandan government officials, was displeased by my reporting. The threats came in the form of phone calls and official "invitations" to "visit" government agents in their offices, where they'd grill me on my sources and ask why I'd submitted these stories.

As one official put it bluntly when he called me in and told me to watch my back, they could take me out at any time. "You hear about people committing suicide by jumping off high rises all of the time," he said. "You think people won't believe you did the same, Yasin? They'll think you did it because you couldn't feed your family. Even your editors will believe you've been living a miserable life since leaving Dubai—miserable enough for you to end things."

He also pointed out that it wouldn't make any difference if I complained about these threats to my editors. "You're just a freelancer," he scoffed. "Your editors won't stand by you. They will discard you. You have no choice but to cooperate."

After another story I wrote about Middle East Consultants, a company owned by the Ugandan president's brother, someone from that company called to issue threats as well. "We can target you," he said. "You are no good. In fact, you are nothing. We know your wife and the school your children go to. Don't you dare write about us."

Though I didn't tell my wife about most of these threats, she received phone calls as well, and pleaded with me to stop writing politically sensitive articles. "What's going to happen to your children if you die tomorrow?" she asked. "What do you get from writing these things, anyway? Certainly not much money."

I confess that I was frightened, not so much for me, but for my family. So for a time I bowed under the pressure, stopped writing incendiary stories, and attempted to keep my head down and make a go of things in Uganda. I tried to be optimistic about our future, listing all of the positives. I had invested in rental properties in Kampala while I was working in Dubai, which brought in a modest income, and I'd bought a small plot of land in the country, hoping to start a commercial farming venture. I'd also found a job working in public relations at a university, where I was among the top-ranking administrators.

As time went by, though, none of this was enough to keep my family afloat. The rental incomes didn't always cover the expenses of maintaining the units. The farm failed due to a combination of untrustworthy workers, weather conditions, and my own inability to oversee things because I had to spend most of every week in university accommodations, since it was too far to commute to my job every day. And the salary I earned—the equivalent of $200 monthly after paying taxes—didn't even cover commuting expenses.

Ultimately, my family and I were thrust into poverty and living in a rural village, in an unfinished house without reliable electricity or running water.

With no indoor bathroom, we had to use a latrine pit outside and bathed with buckets of water. Worst of all, I couldn't pay my children's school fees or assist my father with medical bills.

Ironically, because most of my family was even more impoverished, I was still viewed as prosperous. At least I had a roof over my head and a garden to provide food. This put even more pressure on me as relatives constantly came to me, asking for help to buy food and clothing because they had even less than I did.

No matter how little you have in Uganda, if someone asks for help, you offer what you can. My wife's young nieces moved in with us because their mother couldn't afford to feed and house them. So did one of my uncle's sons. Our three-bedroom house, unfinished as it was, provided shelter for many.

With my responsibilities mounting and no way to improve my situation, I was desperate by the time I saw my father for that last conversation. He saw this, though I'd told him nothing about our dire financial circumstances or the threats being made against my life.

As weak as he was, my father, like my wife, encouraged me to stop writing. "We can't make any changes," he told me. "The world is more complex than you think. All your life, you'll have to be on the run if you keep writing, Yasin. What you must do in this life is take care of your family. You think that today is very scary, but what are you going to do tomorrow? You must leave Uganda. There is nothing more you can do here."

My father and I had often locked horns when I was growing up. He was wrong, I thought, to tell me to stop writing. The more I learned about the plight of migrants and refugees around the world, the more compelled I felt to write about them. My voice might be small, but at least I could do something.

But he *was* right about one thing: I knew I had to leave my homeland again. This time I went to the United States, where my younger brother, Wahab, had been granted asylum as a political refugee and was working as a personal care attendant.

When I arrived in the United States in 2017, Donald Trump had just been elected president. I had come to the U.S. for a writers' conference and hoped to find work. Wrongly, I'd expected that, if I found a job as a journalist, my employer could arrange a work permit, since that's how the process worked when I lived in Dubai and Qatar.

Wahab encouraged me to apply for asylum, which was granted three long years later. During that time, I discovered that Black migrant workers like myself have few legal rights in this country and suffer the same systemic racism, or worse, that has sent the U.S. spinning into political and social turmoil while inspiring the Black Lives Matter movement.

*

One evening, as I drove home from a long day of work as a home health aide, a police cruiser appeared behind me with lights flashing. It was 10 p.m. and the roads were nearly empty. Remembering my friend's warnings to "act harmless" or the police might shoot me, I pulled over with my heart pounding.

The Massachusetts governor, Charlie Baker, had just issued a 9 p.m. curfew across the state, but I'd been working and didn't know that. In the three excruciatingly long minutes it took for the officer to approach my car, I imagined all sorts of reasons why I might have been stopped, and wondered what might happen to me.

When the officer appeared at my window, though, he only had one question: "Essential worker?"

"Yes," I said quickly, and he waved me off without asking for so much as my driver's license. The color of my skin had told me what he needed to know.

Many Black migrants and Black Americans are on the front lines of the coronavirus pandemic, working as caregivers, health care professionals, grocery store workers, delivery people, and other essential providers. We've always done essential work, along with the undocumented immigrants working as field hands and in factories and warehouses to ensure that there's no interruption in the nation's food chain. Yet, too often, we're invisible.

As the challenges of working on the front lines have multiplied, so has the need for migrants. The political rhetoric of politicians who demonize immigrants as dangerous criminals, job stealers, and parasites feeding on tax-funded public assistance contrasts sharply with the reality of how necessary it is for this country to legalize hardworking immigrants to fill these essential jobs. We need to enact political reforms that will mitigate, reduce, and ultimately eliminate the barriers that prevent so many migrant workers from making a living wage, so that immigrants forced out of their countries, often by the actions of their own governments working in tandem with Western countries, are able to make an honest living.

*

This is my personal story of just how elusive the American Dream can be. I share my struggle as I work long shifts as a caregiver and Uber driver to make ends meet while I apply for legal status, hoping to bring my wife and five children—the youngest of whom I still haven't met—to the United States from Uganda, so that my family can be reunited in the country I now call home.

But this is more than just my story. It serves as a clarifying backdrop for the global migrant crisis and a rallying cry for change. Here, I share not only my personal experiences as someone who has to take 3D jobs to survive, but the stories of other migrants I have met along the way as well.

I first heard the term "3D worker" at a conference in Dubai about migrant rights. The term derives from a Japanese phrase, *kitanai, kiken, kitsui,* or 3K, and is typically used to describe certain kinds of jobs considered so dirty, dangerous, and demeaning that most people refuse to take them if they can find something better. These are the sorts of jobs that most Americans hope their children will *not* take, especially if their children have college degrees. Yet, these are the jobs necessary to keep this great nation alive and breathing.

In the U.S., 3D jobs include personal caregivers, Uber/Lyft drivers, and those who work in housekeeping, factories, construction, landscape crews, meatpacking plants, slaughterhouses, and agricultural fields, among others. People in these positions are essential to society, yet they make low wages and often work in uncomfortable, even dangerous conditions. Migrants like me must make daunting decisions to survive, often day-by-day.

By sharing my story and others, I hope to create empathy both for those in 3D jobs and a broader understanding of why migrants keep coming to this country, despite the hardships they face.

In this book, I explore the reasons why Black African migrants like me feel compelled to risk everything to leave our homelands and families for other countries—even when those countries make it abundantly clear that we are not wanted, despite the fact that we are essential to keeping the economies of those countries strong. Sometimes our journeys are risky, or even dangerous. Sometimes, they are depressing and disheartening. Whether we arrive as refugees or migrant workers, most of us suffer great losses as we become separated and fractured from our homelands, cultures, native tongues, and extended families—or even from our own children.

Meanwhile, we walk a tightrope when it comes to fitting in. At times we're praised as "hardworking immigrants" who are following in the footsteps of the immigrants who came here and made America "great," while at other times we're seen an alien invaders intent on "stealing jobs," or, worse, as terrorists and rapists.

Many of us have college degrees or even advanced degrees, while others are skilled artisans. Unfortunately, as migrants we have no choice but to take dirty, dangerous, and demeaning jobs, working twice as hard to prove our worth not only as workers, but also as humans. We are thrust into the front lines as essential workers, especially during times like this one, when the coronavirus pandemic rages around the world.

Despite these hardships, we will keep coming. Throughout these pages, I delve into the historical, economic, and political currents that have served throughout history to carry us to Western shores, and that are still bringing us here now.

Welcome to America

BORIS, my supervisor from the home healthcare agency, had already arrived at the client's house. It was cold out, but not as frigid as when I'd landed in Boston in February. Shortly after my arrival in the U.S., I had made the mistake of walking to the bank wearing only a thin sweater; by the time I stepped up to the counter, I was shivering so hard that the bank clerk noticed.

"Where are you from?" he asked.

"Africa," I said through chattering teeth, thinking longingly of Uganda, of that lush landscape and my house filled with family. Uganda seemed like another planet compared to this city buried in snow, where I shared a damp basement room with my brother.

The bank clerk shook his head. "My God," he said. "I'm going out to buy you a jacket. Stay right here until I get back."

True to his word, he returned minutes later with a warm, puffy jacket. It was the first of many kindnesses I experienced in this strange new land.

It was my first day as a home health aide. I'd dressed neatly in pressed gray slacks and a white shirt. It was more of an academic's outfit, but I didn't own many clothes and wanted to look professional. Even though I'd passed the online Home Health Aide (HHA) course, the training was basic and I worried about being adequately prepared. I'd earned a university degree in communications and an MBA as well, but my previous career in journalism hardly qualified me for medical emergencies.

The agency had said this would be a one-week, live-in position. All I had to do was survive the week, I reminded myself.

Besides, what choice did I have?

"Good morning," I said now, climbing the steps to the client's home, where Boris was waiting for me on the porch. He was a tall white man, built like a greyhound, with a monk's fringe of brown hair.

"Good to see you, Yasin," Boris said. "Thanks for coming. This client is special to our agency. I chose you myself for the job, because I know you'll give a hundred percent of your effort to keeping him comfortable."

"Thank you for the opportunity," I said.

Inside the house, I struggled not to let my jaw drop. I'd been told that the client, Douglas, needed a home health care aide after a stroke left him paralyzed. Nobody had mentioned that the man was massive; he probably tipped the scale at 350 pounds.

Boris and Douglas's wife, Hattie, explained that they wanted me to transfer Douglas manually from his bed to his wheelchair without using the Hoyer lift, which sat in a corner of the bedroom.

"You'll want to use what's called a 'pivotal transfer,'" Boris explained. "That will minimize the lifting weight pressure on your back. Your spinal cord won't be in any danger of injury if you do it right."

"What's the problem with using the Hoyer lift?" I pointed to the device, thinking the machine must be broken.

"We don't want to use it," Hattie explained. "That's why we wanted to hire a male aide who can handle the weight requirements to move my husband."

I expected Boris to talk sense into her—lifting a man of this size would endanger both me and her husband—but he said, "Let's have you move Douglas now, so I can make sure you understand how to do it."

Were they joking? Was this some strange test? I'm in my thirties, a husband and father. I'm neither tall nor muscular; I'm inclined to be more academic than athletic. Plus, I walk with a limp due to a bad knee, the result of polio I suffered as a child. How could I possibly lift this guy?

But I needed this job if I was going to feed my family, so I followed Boris's instructions, raising the bed with a remote control until Douglas was sitting up. Douglas attempted to speak, but his speech was too impaired for any of us to understand him.

I managed to turn Douglas around by grabbing the waistband of his pants and tugging until he faced the edge of the bed with his feet on the floor. Still facing him, I wrapped a transfer belt around the man's huge girth and pushed my own knees against Douglas's legs for leverage as I lifted him into a standing position, holding onto the belt wrapped around his waist for dear life.

Without warning, my bad knee gave way, sending an intense pain shooting up my leg. I bit my lip to keep from crying out and used my back muscles to finish lifting Douglas out of bed rather than cause more injury to my leg. Slowly, I turned him around and lowered him into the wheelchair.

After I'd seated Douglas properly, Hattie and Boris both clapped their hands, as if I'd performed some clever circus trick. "Nice work," Hattie said.

But my command performance was far from over. "Now let's see you transfer Douglas back to the bed," Boris said.

My knee was burning and my back was shrieking. Still, I managed to move Douglas back to the bed— only to be told that now I had to return him to the wheelchair again, where he would sit for the rest of the day.

"Congratulations," Boris said, slapping me on the shoulder.

"Oh, yes, well done!" Hattie beamed.

I didn't want to complain about my pain in front of Douglas and his family, so I waited for the chance to talk with Boris privately, stepping out onto the porch with him as he was leaving.

"Boris, may I have a word?" I said.

"Yes?"

"Look, I'm sorry, but I'm not the right person for this job," I said. "My knee and back are already aching. I can't transfer this man."

"Come on, why would you complain?" Boris scoffed. "The aide who works here on weekends is African, too, and he never complains. You're all very strong!"

I stared at him. Was he actually trying to tell me that all African men were strong? Bad enough that the white secretary at the agency had found out that I was from Africa and said, "Oh, I've always wanted to go to Africa and do a safari. Is your home near animals? I'd love to see lions."

"There are homes here in America with many more animals than mine," I had joked. "We don't see a lot of lions in Kampala. Too many cars and skyscrapers."

"I can't do this job," I insisted to Boris. "I could get hurt, and the patient might, too."

Boris held up his hands. "Okay, okay. I'll find someone to replace you. Until I do, though, you have to stay here. You can't leave. Do you understand?"

I nodded, knowing that I was effectively trapped until Boris set me free.

That night, after changing Douglas' diaper and putting him to bed, I stared at the wall, wondering what my children were doing now. I missed them so profoundly that at times the sorrow filled my throat like cotton.

I missed everything about my old life in Uganda— the Sunday soccer games, the family celebrations, the red dirt roads, the sweet smell of tropical fruits, the birdsong—but I ached for my children most of all. The recent conversation I'd had with my five-year-old daughter, Hadijja, threatened to tear my heart wide open any time I remembered it.

We share a birthday, and when I talked to her that

day, she'd begged me to come home. "Daddy, that way, you can sing 'Happy Birthday' to me, and I can sing it to you, like we used to do together!" she said. "Please, Dad. Come home."

I would if I could, my daughter.

How did I end up here?

I am not a slave, but I am not free, either.

I could see all too clearly how things were deteriorating in Africa, where people are fleeing the continent by the boatload because there is inadequate food and healthcare, the governments are corrupt, and international corporations own the land's resources while Africa's people go hungry.

People in Europe see these boat people as a security threat, just as President Trump spoke of Mexicans as rapists and murderers. With nowhere to go, as Megan K. Stack pointed out in her 2020 profile of Kurdish refugee and journalist Behrouz Boochani in *The New York Times Magazine*, we are living in an age of refugee camps.

"The camps lie scattered throughout the Middle East," she writes, "cluster on Greek islands and stretch like an ugly tattoo along the U.S.-Mexican border. Camps sprawl through Bangladesh, Chad and Colombia."

People are suspended in a "stateless and extralegal limbo," she adds. "Countless individual lives weave into a collective panorama of displacement and state-lessness and detention. These truncated journeys are a defining experience of our times."

Although I wasn't in a refugee camp, thankfully, I was stuck living in limbo until my asylum claim could be processed. The only way for me to survive was to take the most basic jobs, the only jobs open to migrant workers with temporary status.

But I was determined to see this through. More than a million migrants crossed into Europe in 2015, mostly by sea, prompting a refugee crisis of epic pro-portions. Nobody really knows how many refugees have died leaving their countries. Human traffickers don't exactly keep passenger lists. However, I'd read too many stories of bodies found floating in the sea, the bodies of people trying to leave Africa, and I wanted to be certain that my children would never be among them.

*

I couldn't sleep that night at Douglas's house despite my fatigue and aching muscles. I could only count the hours I had remaining in that enormous house.

Time moved at a snail's pace in my new caregiver's role, with periods of intense boredom punctuated by back-breaking work. I was supposed to lift Douglas several times in a day: in the morning from the bed to the wheelchair, at the midday before lunch to change his diapers on the bed. Later, getting him back into his chair for the afternoon, and then lifting him out of the chair and into his bed around 9:30 pm for the evening.

Besides the lifting, my tasks included giving Douglas a sponge bath, cleaning his dentures, and changing his diapers during the day.

"Now, be sure not to put him in a diaper at night, Yasin," Hattie reminded me before bedtime. "Douglas gets skin sores if he wears diapers at night."

If Douglas had a bowel movement at night, she explained, my job was to clean him and change the disposable linens on his bed.

This was a far cry from my old life at the university in Kampala, I thought, remembering one of the last meetings I'd had with the Chancellor, where I'd given him talking points for a radio interview I'd arranged.

That first night, Douglas had such severe diarrhea that I didn't even know where to start. I cleaned and cleaned and cleaned him, struggling to shift his heavy body from one side of the bed to the other so I could wipe up the mess and change his bedding.

This happened twice more in the night. Each time I cleaned Douglas up, I fought to maintain a pleasant expression and continued making small talk, imagining that, no matter how difficult this task must be for me, it had to be terrible for him; he was a wealthy, professional white man who was now as helpless as an infant.

I also thought about how glad I was that I hadn't told my wife anything about the exact nature of the work I was doing. Back home in Uganda, returning migrants who have been abroad taking care of the elderly are called "buttocks washers."

The truth was that I felt for Douglas and the other elderly patients I'd worked with as a home health care aide. Unlike in Uganda, where you are always surrounded by extended family from birth to death, these clients seemed to have nobody in their own families willing to care for them.

Some patients needed to have their diapers changed up to eight times a day due to diarrhea or incontinence. Diaper changes couldn't be delayed, because a soiled garment could trigger infections or severe skin rashes, which would be noticed by examining physicians or nurses looking for bed sores. Added to this, I had to move Douglas's enormous body. My back and bad knee were threatening to give way. I had never felt so diminished or exhausted. What's more, I was terrified that I might somehow drop Douglas if my own body broke down.

In the middle of the night, I felt so despondent

that I wrote a group email to the agency, explaining what I had discussed with Boris and asking the agency to please replace me immediately.

On Tuesday morning, Boris showed up and told Douglas's family that he was doing a routine check. I'd put Douglas in his wheelchair, and when Boris asked how the transfer had gone, Douglas managed to say, "Good work."

I was relieved to hear his answer. I hadn't said anything to Douglas about having trouble transferring him, and it was clear that his family—including a friendly son who was a student at Harvard University—seemed to like the way I was taking care of him.

Afterward, Boris called me outside to the porch, where he chastised me for betraying his trust in African men. "You are a strong race of people," he said. "I'm disappointed that you would complain to the agency about a little hard work. If you want to be replaced, we'll just fire you, and believe me, you'll never be considered for any other openings if that happens."

I was stunned by his threat, but stood my ground. "I'm sorry you feel that way," I said, "but I still can't do this work."

When no replacement arrived from the agency to relieve me of my duties that day, I wrote another group email to the agency, this time saying that I accepted Boris's decision to fire me, adding that they needed to find a replacement for me by the next day, or else I would take matters into my own hands.

This time, the agency owner himself replied with a text on my phone. "If you ever leave a client's home without us finding a replacement for you," he wrote, "I'll file a complaint against you in court, accusing you of abandoning a quadriplegic patient."

It was then that I realized how powerless I really was. Seven months had passed since I filed the claim, and two months since my initial interview. Because I was waiting for my asylum application to be processed, any court case filed against me could be detrimental to my status.

Besides, how would I, a Black migrant worker, ever win a court case against a wealthy white man?

I was trapped.

In the light of this understanding, I remained prudent. I relented and stopped asking to be relieved and reassigned.

On Wednesday, while still at the couple's home, the supervisor again came, this time telling the clients that I had complained about the workload and that I was threatening to discontinue the assignment.

From the room in which I stayed I could hear the wife explaining to the supervisor that they did not believe they had requested tasks excessively. She said the job was principally the transfer of the husband between wheelchair and bed at various times during the day.

After the supervisor left, the family's attitude toward me changed completely and this complicated my work even more, at a time when I had no further options. The client spent most of the time on his computer and when I was on my own in my room I simply stared. I could not read the book I carried nor could I continue on my writings. I just stared. At night I could not even sleep; I only stared and counted the time I had remaining in that house and even that seemed to move at a snail's pace.

I soon learned about my wider situation.

On Thursday, as I had abandoned the idea of leaving the house, the supervisor didn't come, so I chatted with the client's son, who was in his mid-twenties.

"My father is annoyed because he is paying the company $35 per hour for your service and you are complaining," he said.

The son also mentioned they were paying $20 per hour for their personal care assistant, and he never complained about anything. I resisted the urge to tell him that out of the $35 per hour they paid the agency, I was only paid $12 per hour to do the work, far less than their PCA. But that would have sounded like I was protesting the poor pay and not being able to do the heavy lifting.

Friday finally came and I was scheduled to leave the client's house, and I happened to meet the African man who was the PCA on my way out. He appeared to be in his mid- to late-twenties and had a frame that was bulkier and more muscular than mine, sort of like a weightlifter.

My Ugandan Worker

AFTER I had applied for asylum and received a work permit, one of the first jobs I had in Boston was as a personal caregiver for an elderly white couple living on social security. Rachel was sixty-eight years old and had been completely paralyzed since birth due to a spinal cord injury. She spent most of her time in bed unless she needed to be lifted and put into her wheelchair.

Rachel had sparse, feathery white hair like goose down and bright blue, intelligent eyes. She'd worked for the IRS most of her life. Her diminutive size—she weighed only about 90 pounds—was a welcome relief after my week of taking care of Douglas, yet she was still difficult to lift.

Rachel's husband, Tom, had just turned seventy. He and Rachel had met in college.

"He had to take me to the bathroom the first time we met," Rachel confided after I'd known her for a while. "What a first date, right? But I couldn't get into the bathroom on my own and he helped me."

True love comes in all forms, I thought.

Clearly, this couple was intelligent and Tom, at least, had probably come from a family with means; however, they'd both been cut off from their families for years and were totally dependent on caretakers.

"His father literally fainted and died when Tom introduced me to him," Rachel said, "after telling Tom that they didn't want to see him anymore with 'that cripple.'"

Tom was frail after having suffered five strokes and required a walker to get around. He had converted to Islam under the influence of terrorists Tamerlan Tsarnaev and Dzhokhar Tsarnaev, the people who were involved in the Boston Marathon bombing. Katherine Russell, Tamerlan's wife, had worked in this couple's home as Rachel's caregiver, while Tamerlan was hired to take care of Tom. While the couple was working there, they had realized that, since Rachel was bedridden and Tom was so frail, this was the perfect place to prepare the bombs, so I wasn't surprised when one of the first questions Rachel asked was what religion I was.

"Muslim," I said.

Rachel was shocked. "He's Muslim," she shrieked at her husband. "Oh my God, what am I going to do? I don't want any more Muslims!"

"She's afraid of Muslims, but she'll be fine with you," Tom said.

"I never wanted any more Muslims in my house," Rachel declared, then tilted her head and scrutinized me closely. "Yasin, you don't look like a man who would use obscenities. Is that true?"

"That's true," I said. "I'm a good person. Harmless," I added, because that's the word my friend, Musa, had used to describe how I should act with the police.

This proved to be the right answer for Rachel and her husband, who wore a bright red Make America Great cap and was an avid Trump supporter, and a Muslim.

I was hired.

*

With a work permit, it's easy for a migrant to find a job in the U.S. if they're willing to take care of the elderly or the mentally challenged, pick fruit and vegetables, work in the meat-packing industry, clean houses, wash dishes, drive a car for Uber or Lyft, tar roofs, or do any of the other sorts of jobs most U.S. citizens won't take. No matter what our level of education or experience, or how essential these tasks might be, migrant workers are paid hourly and at the minimum wage of $10 to $12 per hour, depending on the state.

Direct caregiving for the elderly and disabled represent the most common employment for Black African migrants, despite the fact that, according to the Pew Research Foundation, Black immigrants from Africa are more likely than Americans overall to have a college degree or higher.

Direct caregiving jobs are easy to find in nursing homes, rehabilitation centers, group homes, and private residences of elderly and disabled people. In Massachusetts, where I live, several direct care agencies recruit workers daily. Direct caregivers are classified under the Fair Labor Standards Act (FLSA) as hourly workers entitled to minimum wage and overtime. The largest group among the direct caregivers consists of Home Healthcare Aides (HHA), who work in private homes. With an increased number of aging and disabled people choosing to stay home, many will need a home health aide at some point if they don't have family members to care for them.

Despite the relative ease of availability, these jobs come with a good deal of responsibility. Direct caregivers are responsible for high-risk elderly people such as those suffering from Alzheimer's, dementia, cancer, Parkinson's, and other chronic and progressive illnesses. A caregiver's tasks often involve tending to the physical needs known in industry parlance as the Activities of Daily Living (ADLs). These include transferring patients safely from bed to wheelchair, toilet access, showers, feeding, and sometimes being able to spot and care for wounds.

And, no matter how serious the responsibilities might be, caregivers are often seen as invisible or irrelevant, even when they bond closely with their charges.

I was hired as Rachel's personal care assistant (PCA). This job technically required at least a certified nursing assistant (CNA) certificate, but I'd never done the CNA classes. CNA certification would require me to attend traditional classes for one month and complete written and practical exams administered at the state level, to the tune of at least a thousand dollars—a thousand extra dollars that I didn't have.

Now, after landing a PCA job without a CNA certificate, I was reluctant to sacrifice the time and money it would take to obtain the certificate. I was still desperately hoping that I was doing the job only temporarily, as I continued searching for a stable, long-term assignment as a journalist—an objective that was sadly becoming increasingly difficult to achieve.

My PCA job with Rachel, like my other HHA jobs, was more like what a housemaid or house boy position would be elsewhere in the world. I did all of the household chores, including vacuuming the carpets, preparing meals, washing dishes, cleaning bathrooms, helping male patients with showers and bathing, changing adult diapers, and giving sponge baths for female patients.

I carried Rachel to her wheelchair, and escorted her to doctor's appointments and other outings, including social dinners and church services.

Despite her physical limitations, Rachel's mind was clear and vigorous, and she considered herself my supervisor. She instructed me to take 30 minutes for a lunch break, and would always start timing my break on her Alexa device immediately after I finished her afternoon diaper change.

While I took my lunch break, Rachel sometimes had a quick nap. She woke up refreshed and ready to issue additional orders. If she was awake during my lunch break, she would send her husband into the kitchen to see me. Tom's job was to remind me of the time.

"Just fifteen more minutes on your break," he'd bark, then, "Ten minutes." And, finally, "Five minutes left on your lunch break, Yasin."

Because Tom usually sat in his bedroom with his metallic walker nearby, I could hear the ominous banging noises of the walker's metal legs coming down the hall to the living room when he came to count down the minutes left in my free half hour. I had to grit my teeth to keep smiling, and reminded myself that Rachel and Tom had nothing else to occupy themselves. I was their entertainment for the day as much as their caregiver.

As the days went by in their employment, I quickly realized that Rachel was uncomfortable spending any time without me beside her. In the morning, I washed her eyes, prepared breakfast, and fed her, then changed her diapers. Then I'd do household tasks until it was time to fix lunch.

Rachel wanted me to stretch her lunch out for as long as possible, even if she was only having yogurt.

"Use a smaller spoon," she'd insist, or she'd take only half a spoonful at a time, so that it took an inordinate amount of time to finish feeding her. If she had bread with butter, I was required to slice the crusts off and cut the bread into tiny slivers.

After lunch, I'd lift Rachel into her wheelchair, at which point she would follow me around the house and keep me on my toes. We might sort out the fridge together, or she'd point out places she wanted me to sweep, vacuum, or scrub. She didn't go to bed until eleven o'clock at night, and I was so exhausted by then that I'd fall into a deep sleep in the room across the hall from hers.

Rachel was clearly eager to see that every paid minute of my time was well-earned. No moment of idleness was allowed in her home, which was why my agency supervisor admitted to me that many workers never returned to Rachel after a single day's work.

Whenever there were no tasks for me to do in the kitchen or living room, Rachel expected me to sit with them to watch television, discuss politics, and share in her gossip about her family, friends, and neighbors. Many of Rachel's conversations revolved around her daughter, Beth, and Beth's Black husband. Rachel didn't approve of their marriage.

In the evenings, Rachel, Tom, and I listened to audiobooks together, and when there was no audio format available, I would read a chapter or two from their books aloud before they went to sleep.

The repetition of chores was numbing. Rachel demanded that I change her diapers every two hours even when they were still clean. When she thought there was no more work for me, she'd ask me to wipe her nose every five minutes. This required removing and replacing her oxygen.

One day, I counted the times I wiped Rachel's nose

between nine a.m. to eleven p.m. I stopped counting at sixty. It wasn't that she had a runny nose; she simply wanted to ensure that I was busy every moment.

Occasionally, I'd say, "Rachel, let's go five minutes without cleaning your nose, shall we? Your nose is so dry!"

"No, my nose is running. You have to wipe it, Yasin!" she'd say.

Again, I tried to be patient, because I knew Rachel was bored and had no other way of having power in the world. This woman had fought to be accepted, to be *seen*, all of her life, just as I was doing now as a Black African migrant worker in the U.S.

"Even my own family has abandoned me," Rachel told me once. "You're the first stranger who's accepted me."

*

Nothing bothered me quite as much as when I took Rachel to doctor's appointments, where she would introduce me to everyone as "my Ugandan worker" in a boastful tone, as if she were reminding other people that she should not be demeaned because she "owned" a worker.

Hearing her say this made me feel slightly sick to my stomach, as if Rachel really did own me—as if I needed permission to do anything she hadn't ordered me to do, which in some ways really did seem to be the case.

The only thing that gave me some small comfort was that the nurses would usually roll their eyes at me, or whisper, "Boy, you've really got your hands full there," whenever they overheard Rachel talking about me in this way.

Rachel texted me, too, when I was at home, to make certain I was coming in the next day. Or, if I had a dentist's appointment, she might text to see if I'd left my apartment yet, or call the dentist to ask if I'd arrived. All of this was irritating, except that I knew Rachel's behavior was driven by her anxiety.

The one place I really drew the line was when she asked me to take selfies of me feeding her so that she could post them on Facebook. I couldn't bear the idea of advertising the low, migrant life I had assumed in America on social media.

I was in Rachel's house for three consecutive days every week. For the other four days of the week, I worked at other jobs. The practice of staying overnight during such work was always called "live in" and was very much sought after by workers because the hours added up.

When Rachel found out that I'd celebrated a birthday, she bought me the book *Uncle Tom's Cabin* by

Harriet Beecher Stowe, the famous novel on the life of slaves in America. Despite the oddity of the gift, I was touched. It's not common to celebrate birthdays in Uganda.

I had already read the book long before meeting Rachel, but as I reread some of the passages in Stowe's book that night at Rachel's house, it reminded me that my life in the U.S. can never compare to the misfortunes of slaves in 1800s. Yet, I still despaired at feeling trapped in a life of servitude. I couldn't even imagine what it must be like for the Black migrant workers who came to this country with no education and no hope of achieving legal status; at least I had some chance of having my asylum approved. I was clinging to the hope that soon I'd be granted legal status and be able to bring my family to the U.S.

Rachel seemed determined to talk about the subject of slavery with me, and was always quick to point out how lucky I was to live now instead of back when there were "real" slaves. At one point, she asked me to take her to a movie theater to see *Harriet*, the powerful film based on Harriet Tubman's life.

Afterward, Rachel said, "Well, at least slavery ended long ago."

"Slavery hasn't ended," I said, only partly joking. "It has just evolved. If I went to my grave today and told my slave ancestors that I was a freeman, not a slave like them, they would laugh at me and choke to death. They would say, 'Grandson, let's go through this checklist with you: You lived and worked in a foreign land, yes. You missed home but couldn't go back, yes. You did the same work (3D's) as we did in the 1800s, yes. You worked multiple jobs to afford the basics of livelihood like accommodation and food, while in the 1800s we did just one job and had a single boss, yes. In the 1800s we worked from sunrise to sunset about 10 to 12 hours a day, and you are working day and nights shifts about 18 hours a day, yes. And you believe those assurances from the white man that slavery ended?"

At that point, Rachel did what she always did when she couldn't win an argument: she changed the subject.

*

Rachel was terrified of dying alone, despite having a daughter with Tom. She worried constantly about me being deported.

"If you leave me, I won't have anyone," she said, and suggested that she could contact Massachusetts U.S. Senator Edward J. Markey on my behalf, and that he would be able to get me a green card. This process would require a senator to initiate a private bill on my behalf. Such an option is extremely rare; fewer than 100 immigrants receive such consideration annually.

"Thank you, Rachel, but there's no chance that would happen," I said.

"There's no harm in trying," she insisted. "But, if I do this for you, Yasin, you have to promise to stay with me until I die."

"Let me think about it," I said.

The subject of my immigration status was always on Rachel's mind. I often overheard her discussing the topic with friends, saying that she was worried about losing me and being "thrown into a nursing home."

Just before I'd started working for her, Rachel had spent two months at a rehabilitation center, and she feared returning there. She would tell her friends that she wanted to help me get a green card so that wouldn't happen. Her friends would caution her, explaining that there were no guarantees.

"There's every chance Yasin will leave as soon as he gets a green card," one friend said.

"If he disappears after my helping him to get a green card, then that would be World War III," Rachel declared.

These humiliating conversations were often carried out in my presence, but my pleas for her to stop fell on deaf ears. Her friends always wanted updates, and Rachel's church even started including my name on their weekly newsletters, imploring church goers to pray for me to get a green card.

I was increasingly desperate for a green card, because I couldn't travel without one, but I didn't want to promise to stay with Rachel. Although we were starting to form a better understanding, being her personal care attendant was grueling and often demeaning.

On the other hand, I missed my children, and they were missing me, too. I couldn't travel anywhere until my asylum was granted; it was looking likely that they'd have to miss me for many more years to come. I was exhausted just thinking about all of the hurdles I still had to leap over or break through to be reunited with my family.

*

One of Rachel's friends suggested that me being a Muslim was the cause of the delay in my asylum being granted. I wasn't from any of the six Muslim countries that President Trump had elected for a travel ban (later replaced with stricter vetting). However, it's true that the general acceptance rate of Muslim asylum applications plummeted from 40,000 in 2016 to 8,000 in 2018, a cut of 80 percent.

Never mind the fact that discrimination on the basis of religion or race violates this country's Constitution. The Trump administration made improving relations with the Saudi monarchy its foremost foreign policy, with President Trump visiting the rich Gulf state first. How ironic is it that U.S. immigration policies target impoverished Muslims, while Washington is in bed with the worst dictators in Muslim countries, like King Salman of Saudi Arabia?

However, on my more optimistic days, I was inclined to believe that the delay in my asylum process was simply an indication of the contradictions inherent in the U.S. immigration policy: politicians want migrants to "get legal," then make it nearly impossible for them to do so.

According to the National Conference on State Legislatures (NCSL), in FY 2018, 22,491 refugees were admitted to the U.S.– that's a massive 58 percent drop from 53,716 admitted in 2017. Little wonder, then, that many immigrants see phony marriage as the only viable route to legalize their stay in this country, or that the cost of such a marriage has shot up from $10,000 during President Obama's Administration to almost $30,000 in the Trump era. But the marriage route is also fraught with challenges, including the risk of abuse and the ordeal of scrutiny. Women are especially vulnerable.

For instance, a Ugandan coworker at a group home for people with developmental disabilities told me how her arranged marriage turned sour. It involved a Haitian man and cost $25,000, $10,000 of which she paid in cash to start the process, with the balance to be paid in monthly installments.

The man proposed they rent a house to look more convincing. After a few days, the man demanded sex, and because she owed him a lot of money, my coworker consented. When she became pregnant, he demanded that she get an abortion, but she refused. Unfortunately, a few months after they had the baby, the man successfully brought a young bride from Haiti. Now my colleague had no choice but to pursue an asylum claim, which meant paying more money to an immigration lawyer.

The bottom line is that achieving the American Dream through fake marriage is an expensive exercise that costs not only a lot of money, but also a person's dignity. Migrants sell everything they have in order to get to the U.S., only to realize that we will have to make more sacrifices. We work day and night for years to pay to have the opportunity for a legal stay in this country.

None of that will stop us from coming.

The problem is not actually immigration, as the

politicians and corporate moguls of the West have brainwashed many Western citizens into believing through their corporatized media. President Trump has himself pointed out that he would be glad to welcome migrants from Norway. The problem is nationalism. Europeans and their American cousins are becoming ever more protective of the global wealth they have been collecting across the planet for centuries.

*

In one of my other caregiver jobs before being hired by Rachel, I worked at a nursing home. During the night, one of my patients died, and I called his son.

"I'm so sorry to have to tell you, but your father has passed away," I said.

"Oh, Dad died?" the son said. "Okay. Thanks. Can you call me in the morning and tell me where they took the body?"

"Of course," I said, but after I hung up the phone, I sat there, feeling stunned. I couldn't imagine being able to sleep if my father's body was about to be taken away and put into a refrigerator. It's difficult for me to imagine how lonely it must be to live without family, and how absolutely terrifying it must be to die alone. This would never happen in Uganda. Our extended families gather around the elderly and dying. We are never alone when we leave this world.

Americans shouldn't be left to die alone, either. Nor should they be forced into nursing homes if they can live at home with help.

Yet, many elderly U.S. citizens will be institutionalized at great cost to their families and the government, and many will die alone, if legislation isn't passed to allow more migrant workers to enter the country and serve as caregivers.

According to a recent CNN report, a whopping 75 percent of Americans over 65 live with multiple chronic health conditions, ranging from diabetes to dementia. The country's healthcare system will collapse as it tries to keep sick seniors out of hospitals, assisted-living facilities, and nursing homes and instead have them cared for in their homes, because there is a severe shortage in health care aides. With 10,000 baby boomers in the U.S. turning 65 each and every day, our aging population will double in the next 20 years. Experts estimate that the overall employment of in-home aides is projected to grow 41 percent from 2016 to 2026 — resulting in 7.8 million job openings.

Who is going to fill those jobs?

The healthcare system is broken in the U.S., and nothing has shone a brighter light on its many fissures than the global pandemic—a factor that has caused even *more* older Americans to want to avoid nursing homes, because that's where the virus spreads like wildfire.

The home healthcare industry shines a harsh light on immigration issues. According to the Migration Policy Institute (MPI), in 2018 more than 2.6 million immigrants, including 314,000 refugees, were employed as healthcare workers. As a group, immigrant healthcare workers are more likely than their U.S.-born counterparts to have university-level educations. Relative to their share of the total workforce, immigrants make up disproportionate shares among both high- and low-skilled healthcare workers. According to MPI, immigrants accounted for 38 percent of the 492,000 home health aides in the U.S. in 2018.

To date, foreign-born healthcare workers have arrived in the U.S. under a variety of temporary and permanent visa categories. Temporary visa categories include H-1B (specialty occupations), TN (Mexican and Canadian professionals under the North American Free Trade Agreement [NAFTA]), J-1 (exchange visitors), O-1 (persons with "extraordinary ability or achievement"), and E-3 (specialty occupation workers from Australia), according to the MPI. As is the case with other immigrants, those in the healthcare sector can be admitted through permanent immigration channels (i.e., getting a green card) based on family or employment connections, or through humanitarian protection routes.

Now that pipeline of essential workers to the U.S. is closing tighter and tighter.

Looking only at the number of African refugees and asylum seekers to this country, according to Homeland Security estimates for proposed and actual refugee admissions, in 2017 there was a ceiling of 35,000 refugees from Africa, with 20,232 being admitted to the U.S. In 2018, those numbers dropped precipitously to a ceiling of 19,000 refugees, with only 10,459 being admitted under President Trump.

If anti-immigrant sentiments continue to be fanned and fester, and federal policies to severely restrict immigration remain in place, many more elderly Americans will be institutionalized and will die alone.

*

Even when you are in despair, even when you think you cannot rise one more day to do the work you must do, time passes, and there are always some good days among the bad.

As I continued working with Rachel and Tom, my relationship with them deepened and our understanding of one another grew. They bought and read my two previously published books and, like many other people, were flabbergasted that circumstances had caused me to flee my country and work as a caregiver despite my education and previous journalism career.

Rachel started calling me "the brother I never had," and asked me to call her "Mummy" because she was almost the same age as my mother. She began buying gifts for my children on each of their birthdays, though most of the dolls she sent them were never delivered because of the poor postal services in Uganda.

It was clear that Rachel trusted me as much as she'd ever trusted anyone. I was her first call and reference in any emergency, regardless of whether I was at work or not. And, whenever the ambulances arrived to take her to the hospital in an emergency, Rachel would insist they call me. I accompanied her to the hospital even when I wasn't on the job.

Rachel started calling me twice a day, and if I was busy on another job and didn't pick up, she'd become extremely worried. She would ask all her friends and her daughter to send me text messages asking me to call her back. Sometimes I'd receive as many as five texts from different people.

Whenever I called Rachel back, she'd typically have nothing much to tell me. "I just wanted to make sure you're coming back next week," she might say.

We had lively discussions over slavery and immigration as we became more comfortable with one another. One day, we were discussing Africa and the high unemployment levels there, and Rachel said, "At least you're here now. Africans should be grateful to be in the U.S. where they can at least get jobs."

This is the assumption most Americans make about migrant workers: that we should be grateful for any sort of work we can get in this country. It's true that we are happy to be working—that is why we have come, after all, to make better lives for ourselves—but I couldn't help myself. I had to ask Rachel if she thought she'd want her own daughter to work as a caregiver and do for someone else what I did for her.

Rachel looked appalled. "My God, no," she said. "My daughter has a college degree!"

"Well, so do I," I said. "And an MBA besides."

"Still, at least Black people in the U.S. can get good jobs if they work really hard," Rachel insisted. "Look at Oprah."

I laughed. "How many Black people do you know who have their own TV shows?"

She shook her head then, and told me about a Nigerian caregiver she'd had before I started working with her. "He was a doctor back in Nigeria," she said. "Can you believe he did this job?"

"Of course," I said. "This is where all migrant

workers have to start, and we all are very likely to do this kind of work for a very long time before we can realize our dreams. We arrive with strong ambitions, intent on making something of ourselves, but after some time, you realize this is all that's available to you."

There was a brief silence as Rachel thought about this. Then she said, "Well, I think that doctor should be grateful to have a job in America. You should be, too."

I went to bed thinking about this. Of course I was grateful for any opportunities I had in this country. At the same time, the road ahead seemed impossibly long and twisted, with no certain outcome.

Even the most accomplished Black migrant workers I knew faced this same treacherous odyssey. For example, Faisal Kikomeko graduated as a medical doctor from Makerere University Kampala Uganda in 2006. He completed his residency in Mukono and started practicing in Nsambya Hospital in Kampala.

His dream was to work in one of America's hospitals alongside the brightest brains in medicine. To that end, he applied for several U.S. residencies, but was never accepted. Then, in May 2012, he was one of two doctors sent from Uganda to a medical workshop in Chicago. Once he'd arrived, he knew he wouldn't go back to Uganda—in fact, most of the other African doctor trainees at that conference, from Kenya, Cameroon, Nigeria, Zimbabwe, and Ghana were also planning to stay in America and find work as physicians or enroll in school.

A relative of his wife's offered to put him up in Chicago after the workshop. Reality started sinking in when Kikomeko realized the long road ahead to practice medicine in the U.S., where all foreign-trained doctors are required to take the U.S. medical licensing exam, be certified by the Educational Commission of Foreign Trained Medical Graduates, enter a residency program, and pass the third licensing test. The process was long and costly, with all expenses to be paid by Faisal, who wasn't working.

He needed about $25,000 for the whole process. After consulting with friends, he decided to go to Boston, find an entry job as a caregiver, and save the money to pay for the exams and its preparations.

It took Kikomeko three years to work and pay the required fees for the exams. Unfortunately, he was working so many hours as a caregiver to save the money that he failed to pass the exams on the first attempt. He felt rejected, even traumatized, and decided to put his quest on hold. He talked to his medical colleagues from other countries who had arrived with him, and only one was still on course to be licensed. The other three had changed course and pursued training in nursing. They advised him also to do an LPN or RN, but Kikomeko decided that attaining a permanent residency status in the U.S. would be his next priority.

He had applied for asylum, but three years went by without him even being invited for an interview. The backlog keeps many applicants waiting five years or more just to have an asylum interview. Eventually, Kikomeko decided to abandon the asylum application and pursue a Green Card through marriage instead.

Even back in 2015, arranged marriages were expensive, costing up to $15,000. Most of Kikomeko's energy went into working as many hours as he could to raise the money. Finally, after being granted his marriage Green Card in 2016, he made his first trip back to Uganda to see his family, which included a wife, two children, and his own parents. It was an emotional reunion and his mother somehow convinced him to stay in Uganda and practice medicine again, since his medical license was still valid.

Kikomeko set up a private clinic in Kampala and took an extra job at a big hospital. He worked in Uganda for most of that year, but found himself feeling out of place. He was making very little money for the hours he was working, and so he decided to return to the U.S. He also decided to study for the U.S. medical licensing exams to give it another try.

In 2019, he passed the first exams. He was expecting to do the last exams in 2020 and then pursue a U.S. medical residency, but Covid-19 derailed his plans. Meanwhile, he and his wife are still caregivers for now, just as I am, and probably will be for a long, long time.

*

Then came the pandemic, and new tensions in Rachel's home. Despite our efforts to keep her out of the hospital, we couldn't do it. Rachel's anxiety levels increased, and her panic attacks resulted in her being taken to the hospital every two weeks or so. She worried about contracting Covid-19 there, or from one of her aides, because several of us were also working in risky places like nursing homes.

"I'm worried I'll run out of workers," Rachel fretted.

She was right to worry. The caregiving field has struggled to recruit young people, and many available aides are themselves elderly.

One day, as I was finishing my shift with Rachel, she received a call from the agency saying that they couldn't find a caregiver to work a seven-hour shift the next day. The agency advised Rachel to arrange her own daytime help, perhaps a relative. The earliest they could send someone would be in the evening.

This kind of call wasn't unusual even before the pandemic, despite the fact that Rachel's agency was one of the state's largest suppliers of personal care assistants—many of whom are immigrants. The problem is that Rachel didn't have anyone to turn to for help.

As I arranged my bags to leave, Rachel begged me to find an hour in my schedule the following day to come and just give her food. I agreed, though I'd already been with her for three days straight. I hated the thought of her being alone.

Rachel's anxiety about Covid-19 had begun keeping her awake at night, too, which meant that I was also awake, because she would call me to come in from the next room. If I didn't hear her calling for some reason, she'd ask Tom to wake me.

Tom would wake me by banging his walker on the door of my bedroom. The sound was louder than the school bell that used to wake me up in boarding school. After that, he'd go into Rachel's room, and if I wasn't there within one minute, he'd shuffle back across the hall and bang on my door with his walker again.

There was another development with Rachel, too, as the global pandemic ranged: her anxiety ramped up to the point where she feverishly asked me the same repetitive questions every day, until my own blood pressure skyrocketed and my head pounded. It might go something like this:

"Do you think I had a heart attack?"

"No, Rachel, you didn't have a heart attack," I'd assure her. "You're just feeling nervous, so your heart is beating extra fast."

"What if I have a heart attack?"

"You're not going to have a heart attack."

"Are you going to leave me? What about if you get your green card? If you leave me, are they going to throw me away in a bad nursing home?"

I was never sure who "they" might be, but I'd reassure her that she wasn't going to be put in a nursing home, even though I had no idea if this was true or not.

"What will happen to me if I don't go to the bathroom?" was another frequent question, setting off a round of queries about her bodily state and my reassurances that all problems have a solution, even though I wasn't certain that was true, either.

Rachel's questions about her health and future could go on for hours, with me assuring her she was going to be fine. By the end of these sessions I'd be wrung out.

The other impact of Covid-19 was that Tom could no longer attend any of his day programs. He was stuck in the house now with Rachel and me or another aide. He began showing the stress of lockdown by suffering from anger and depression.

Most of the work done by myself and other aides took place in the bedroom with Rachel. If a meal had to be prepared, within minutes Rachel would tell Tom to go to the kitchen and see what the aide was doing, to ensure that the aide returned to the bedroom to serve her as soon as the kitchen tasks were completed. As Tom watched over the kitchen, he often got into fights with workers over small things, like putting the food in the oven before it preheated.

One day, I was working somewhere else and received five phone calls from Rachel that I couldn't pick up. Finally I received a text from one of Rachel's friends saying there was an emergency. As soon as I got a break, I called Rachel, who told me that Tom had gotten violent and hit a Haitian aide with a chair, accusing her of breaking the microwave. Rachel had been so scared during the altercation that she'd pushed her Lifeline button on the bracelet she wore and asked them to call the police.

Tom became increasingly violent the longer he was forced to remain in the house. At one point, he came into the kitchen where I was preparing lunch, grabbed a saucepan, and tried to hit me with it.

"You dirty Haitians are dumb, stupid, dirty Black

idiots! Why is this country letting you across the border!"

Tom often used the word "Haitian" to refer to any Black immigrants, including me, despite the fact that he'd read my books and knew I was from Uganda. Though I understood that Tom's mood swings weren't anything he could control, I found his increasingly violent behavior disturbing and told Rachel so.

"I'm sorry, Rachel, but I'm not sure I can stay here if this goes on," I said. "I don't mean to stress you out, but if this happens again, I'm gone."

Rachel was definitely stressed. The next day, I got a call saying that she was again being taken to the hospital. While she was there, her daughter Emily sent me a text, saying, *Sorry. I heard my dad wasn't very nice the other day. Thanks for all your kindness to our family and patience.*

When Rachel was home again, I went in for my usual shift, and Rachel called her daughter, pleading with her to talk to Tom. "Your father's going ballistic, calling workers dumb stupid idiots, and saying we shouldn't have them here. I'm not going to have any help if he keeps doing that."

"First, find out why he's behaving that way," Emily said. "There must be a reason, and that's what the workers have to address."

Rachel was talking to her daughter by speakerphone; I could tell from the tone of Emily's voice that she was surprised that her mother was even complaining on behalf of workers.

I went into the kitchen so I wouldn't have to listen and sat with my head in my hands, closing my eyes as if that could shut out not only this conversation, but all of the problems raging in the world outside.

*

In April 2022, my 72-year-old neighbor in Boxborough, Massachusetts, was found dead in his apartment. He lived one door away from me in a sprawling (or better adjective??) apartment complex. Before I learned of his passing, I had noticed an odor that became more foul with each day. Then I had spotted two bowls of strong air freshener placed outside his door and a handwritten notice from the property management explaining that the unit was "sealed shut with weather strip tape" and off limits.

Still unsure of what happened, I asked another neighbor who was walking her dog. She told me that the neighbor had been dead in his apartment for at least ten days and wondered how I did not notice. She said that his body was discovered when his doctor asked the police to check on his welfare because he had missed two appointments. He was found on the floor in his kitchen, his hands clutching the mail he had collected on the day that he died.

My neighbor, a polite white man, had cancer. A month before he died, he told me that he had just finished another round of chemotherapy. He struggled to climb the stairs while clutching two bags of laundry. I offered to help him carry them to the third floor, and he handed over one of the bags. I could still see him struggling with the remaining bag, as he grasped the stairway railing, but he did not allow me to carry both. Once we reached his apartment, we chatted for a few moments. I asked him why he did not have a home health care aide, and he explained that he could not afford one. I had helped him before by taking him grocery shopping, a time when I learned that his wife was in a nursing home.

Previously, as a caregiver I had personally attended to a senior citizen approaching her death. Patricia, an 80-year-old cancer patient, lay in her bed struggling to speak. "She's saying she doesn't want me to leave," I told the nurse. "She thinks that if I leave, she will die."

She was assigned to home-based hospice care due to the cancer ravaging her body, She'd also had a stroke and her speech was badly impaired. I was her Home Health Aide and I had called her nurse when she had a medical emergency.

The nurse noticed that Patricia was smiling as I spoke, and said, "Oh, she's smiling, so she understands fully what we are talking about."

Patricia died a few minutes later, while I held her now-cold hand, reassuring her that she should stay calm and that her journey to the next world would be peaceful.

After Patricia died, her surviving family members were notified, along with the local police and fire authorities. When they arrived, they initially ignored me, as most people ignore caregivers, but the nurse kept redirecting their questions toward me.

Patricia's children didn't invite me to the funeral, but they kept calling me to gather details about her last moments as they prepared her eulogy. I was struck by how they treasured even the smallest details about their mother's life, and found myself wondering what it must be like to die alone in a country like Japan, which has blocked migrants like me from coming, and where there are so few caregivers that many of Japan's elderly are dying alone.

NLI Research Institute, a Tokyo think tank, estimates that about 30,000 people nationwide die this way each year in Japan. Their bodies are sometimes discovered several weeks after they have passed, after their mailboxes fill up or they fall behind on their rent, or when the smell draws attention to their home.

Local newspapers in Japan are full of reports of solitary death. This phenomenon is known as *kodokushi*. A *New York Times* report in late 2017 summarized the phenomenon:

"A single-minded focus on economic growth, followed by painful economic stagnation over the past generation, had frayed families and communities, leaving them trapped in a demographic crucible of increasing age and declining births. The extreme isolation of elderly Japanese is so common that an entire industry has emerged around it, specializing in cleaning out apartments where decomposing remains are found."

As the number of lonely deaths has grown, so too has Japan's lonely-death-cleanup industry. Numerous firms offer this kind of service, and insurance companies have started selling policies to protect landlords if their tenants die inside their properties. The plans cover the cost of cleaning the apartment and compensate for loss of rent. Some will even pay for a purifying ritual in the apartment once the work is done.

Some elderly in Japan are so desperate for assistance, stability, and community that they commit minor crimes so they can spend the rest of their lives in prison. Japan is constructing special prison wards just for elderly inmates to address the record number of crimes committed by senior citizens. With the elderly crime rate nearly quadrupling over the past two decades, around 20 percent of women in prisons are now senior citizens. In most instances, the crime they commit is generally minor and petty, usually shoplifting. For them, living the remainder of their lives behind bars is a better alternative to being alone in their homes. In 2017, a Japanese government survey revealed that over half of all elderly people caught shoplifting said they lived by themselves, while 40 percent claimed they did not have any close relatives.

With the current nationalistic fervor to keep immigrants out of many countries, including the U.S., I fear that this will be an increasingly common occurrence.

Inside the Group Homes

ONE night, a friend called me at midnight in a panic because one of the residents in the group home where he was a caregiver had fallen down the basement stairs.

"I'm running away," my friend said. "If the police come, I'm done. How will I explain this?"

"Calm down," I said. "You can't run away! That will make things so much worse. Where is this person?"

"He's lying on the ground and he's bleeding."

"Call an ambulance, for God's sake!" I said.

"I can't do that. They're going to arrest me if I call an ambulance! Then I'll never get my Green Card! What if I fix him myself?"

"You can't fix him," I said. "Call the ambulance. Accidents happen. I promise nothing will happen."

Eventually that's what my friend did, and the outcome was fine: his client was patched up and my friend kept his job as a residential counselor at a group home.

Group homes across America have replaced the prison-like institutions where people with mental illnesses were kept previously. The facilities, most of which are part of developmental disabilities rehabilitation centers, are recognizable in the sense that they are used by the state as a dumping ground for categories of people in which they are not interested.

There is little funding for these facilities; they survive mostly because of their (cheap) immigrant workforce, which always is understaffed. There is no political will to invest in the institutions or the people who work in them. Politicians simply want governments to spend only the minimum to keep this workforce alive and working. There is little understanding among the political classes about the conditions for patients and workers alike, who neither will or can vote.

Immigrants work in many roles: as residential counselors, teaching assistants, or supervisors, which means taking care of patients round the clock and doing almost exactly the same tasks as when working as a home health aide.

Employers routinely mention a high school diploma as a minimum requirement but then fail to ask the applicant for documents or proof of educational attainment. They only offer 1-2-week courses in the relevant disciplines—the proper use of restraints in emergencies, medical management, First Aid, and so on.

Like other immigrants, I have worked in one of these group homes or schools for people with mental health disorders or those who are developmentally disabled. I took a position at a group home for children from 14–22 where the shift started at 11 p.m. and ended at nine the following morning. Most Ugandans, including me, prefer to work night shifts, a preference that appeals to many employers.

While in most group homes the staff slept on sofas or chairs, especially those with adult clients, sleeping was completely forbidden in the home I worked for, a rule that extends to most group homes with children or teenaged patients.

Surveillance cameras were evident, but they were rarely checked unless an incident occurred.

Since most staff worked multiple shifts and more than 15 hours a day at these *No Sleep* homes, they had to devise a means of catching an occasional power nap. They would avoid detection by studying the surveillance camera angles. This allowed them to put a blanket or cape over their heads while in chairs with their backs facing the camera.

Some bolder staff would catch a quick nap on sofas. Actually, they never checked the cameras regularly, only when there was a fight and staff needed to restrain a patient who had become too violent or aggressive. So, if a staff member slept at night, that person also likely prayed that no young person misbehaved enough to warrant a restraint and a subsequent review of video footage.

I was working both day and night to get more hours and pay. Most nights I would stay awake, reading or writing on my laptop. The most challenging task for the night shift was waking up young people and preparing and driving them to school in the morning rush hours. After staying awake for the full night, one understandably would not be comfortable driving in the morning traffic.

If you were caught sleeping, the punishment was immediate and severe.

A female colleague who had been with the facility for more than five years was abruptly terminated because she was found asleep. A newly hired overnight female staffer found her sleeping in her chair at around two am. The newcomer didn't know that most staffers always found ways to nap in their chair, so she decided to report the incident. She came initially to me so I could be her witness. I replied that it was the role of surveillance cameras to watch over staff members, and mine was to oversee the young patients.

A few minutes after the incident had been reported, the night supervisor—a young Ugandan man—called me asking to wake the sleeping staff member. He wanted to avoid having to make a report that could lead to her dismissal. I told him I couldn't do it because the new staffer was watching everyone.

When he arrived, the sleeping staffer was woken by the doorbell and so it seemed as though it would be ok. But the supervisor relayed bad news: the CEO had called and asked him to relieve the sleeping staffer of her duties. According to protocol, she had to leave the house immediately and the supervisor was supposed to take her seat for the night.

I was struck by how easy it was to fire an immigrant worker in the U.S. without a hearing or indeed any opportunity to consider the circumstances.

The fired staffer, after learning her fate, said she was praying that they don't describe her sleeping on her employee profile as "neglect," because that was considered an abuse of children's rights. Thus, in any attempt to find new employment, she would fail background checks and might not be able to land a job even in a retail or grocery store. That is how risky it was.

Another female colleague quickly found trouble in an interaction with one of the young people, a 17-year-old male. He stood in front of her as if he wanted to ask for something but instead, he spat in her face. She responded with the natural and unconsidered reaction of slapping him; she burst into tears as soon as she realized what she had done.

The whole thing lasted less than a minute but the damage to her employment status already was irreversible. She was terminated and banned from working in any human services setting anywhere in the U.S.

The most challenging moments came when dealing with violent, young patients. Unlike adults, the younger patients had volatile mood changes. Whereas one moment they may be playful, they could be violent and dangerously impulsive in the next. In the case of a display of violent behavior, staff were required to restrain the patient on the floor and allow the mood to pass.

In the home where I worked, one patient, about 20 years old, frequently acted violently towards fellow patients and the staff. If the incident involved another patient, staff were instructed to separate them and to restrain the one who instigated it. An incident report would be followed up by an investigation.

It was not always easy to chronicle the events in the reports, because they happened so quickly and they often involved retaliation between the patients, and so were quite complex interactions. Before a staff member jumped in to separate them, one could see the marks on both individuals.

Investigations often would conclude that the staff did not act quickly enough nor in a sufficiently compassionate manner towards the patient who started the scuffle. In most cases, it was easier to fire and replace a staff member rather than complete an investigation that accurately captured and documented everything that had occurred in the incident.

So, when a patient who had previously been involved in a violent incident approached another patient in a situation that could escalate quickly, the on-duty staff member's anxiety level skyrocketed.

Likewise, scuffles between patients and staff members were even worse, and some staff members acted unprofessionally. In such instances, staff members would be fired and then either prosecuted or deported, depending on whether they had violated the conditions of their immigrant status.

Even if a staff member avoided being deported the incident would go on his/her record, indicating that they had abused a child with special needs. Thus, the migrant would find it extremely difficult if not impossible to land employment wherever criminal background checks were conducted prior to hiring.

Staff members bore the burden of ensuring that the number of violent incidents involving patients were minimized, not least because the group home administration saw every patient's presence as a source of revenue. The cost per patient staying at the home was around $250,000 annually, equivalent to the annual salary of eight staff members.

However, the needs of any given patient could easily prove more than a one-to-one ratio could bear. For example, one day a violent patient attacked a white house manager and bit him on the shoulder, and the victim was taken away bleeding in an ambulance. Had he bitten a black staff member, the administration would have left the incident unreported and unresolved.

One night, a Ugandan male colleague was asked to leave the work premises after getting into an altercation with a frequently violent patient. There were three staff members on duty: my colleague was on the middle level (first floor); I was on the upper (second floor); and there was a Haitian man on the ground floor.

At around three a.m., the student started screaming aloud, demanding to talk to his mom because he could not sleep. I could hear my colleague on the top floor trying to calm him, but the patient responded with ever louder screams. We were not supposed to leave our designated floors until the person attending the patient specifically asked for help, so I stayed on my floor. But the noise grew louder, to the extent that it was waking the patients on my floor.

I realized the house was about to go into meltdown, so I went downstairs briefly to consult my colleague. I found both of my colleagues both trying to restrain the patient on the floor in the hope that he would eventually calm down, so I assisted them, restraining his legs by placing my weight on his knees. I noticed that the Ugandan's glasses were broken.

Finally, the patient calmed down and the Haitian worker asked me to contact the overnight supervisor and report the incident while they continued restraining the student. After calling the supervisor, I returned to my own floor and the other patients returned to their beds.

The supervisor arrived after the patient had become calm.

Both of my colleagues gave different accounts of the incident and the supervisor asked each to write his own report. The Haitian worker claimed he found my Ugandan colleague fighting with the patient in his room, away from the cameras, and had not bothered to even call for backup or staff support in restraining him, which would have been the normal procedure.

Meanwhile, the Ugandan colleague in his report said the patient invited him to his room to fix a radio and suddenly started punching him, which caused his eyeglasses to shatter. He said that he did not fight back but only wanted to defend himself from being injured. The latter account was definitely inaccurate as I had clearly heard the patient demanding to see his mother *before* the altercation. Likely the patient attacked him in the face and broke his glasses and he retaliated.

Also, the patient had some bruises on his face and the supervisor demanded to know what caused them.

As a result of the incident and the inconclusive follow-up, the supervisor called her bosses, read to them both reports and returned with orders for the Ugandan colleague to leave the group home immediately.

I had stayed out of the crisis for most of the night, just observing more staff members arriving and calling for an ambulance to take the patient to the hospital.

But in the morning, I started getting calls. The Ugandan colleague wanted to know what had transpired when he left at night and then instructed me about what I should say to investigators if they called me as a witness.

He wanted me to tell them something like the following: "I was a witness. He did not beat the student; that the Haitian was confused, that he had called for backup, and the Haitian arrived earlier than me because I had a knee injury and could not be quick to arrive on the scene." The way he wanted me to account for the events was akin to "save me first and we shall see what to do for you if you are implicated with your tricky knee."

Instead of investigators from the school calling me, it was the police, so I knew that the incident was being taken seriously. I told the police how little I had been involved in the crisis; just coming onto the scene to help restrain the patient and call the supervisor. It seemed likely that the police called me at the same time as they spoke to my Ugandan colleague because a few minutes after their call, I saw his number come up on my phone as an incoming call.

Tired of the fiasco and desperate for sleep, I ignored the call and switched my phone to silent mode. He called my brother and asked for our home address, telling him he wanted to tell me what to tell the police in case they called again and that he was coming with some Ugandan elders to advise me to stick to the script.

My brother later told me he gave him the address

after noticing he was in a real panic. Eventually, the former staff member was taken to court.

Being understaffed at night was problematic. For example, most patients were assigned a one-to-one ratio with staff during the day but at night that would grow to four-to-one. The group home's management assumed that the violent patient would sleep at night, but that was not always the case.

He would stay up from two until dawn, and almost all the staff on all the other floors would have to abandon their areas to concentrate on taking care of him as he became more violent if he couldn't sleep. Sometimes it was because the day staff had put him to bed earlier—the rules were to let him sleep after nine p.m., but on occasion they would let him go to bed as early as seven because they were relieved when he slept. But, on those days, he also was likely to be awake after midnight and trouble the night staff.

Everyone who worked at that group home tried to avoid the floor on which the violent patient lived. The best ways to avoid it was always to come early and take the topmost floor. The ground floor was always reserved for the young woman who also worked at the house for overnight. Sometimes I would come in as much as an hour early in an effort to avoid the troubled "first floor," but still there were a couple of times when I was slated to work there and there was no getting out of it.

On such nights I relied on prayers that the troubled patient would sleep or at least remain calm if he did wake. If he woke, I would even give him my laptop so he could play games (which was not allowed) to keep him occupied and stop him from fighting. But there were times when he was temperamental, and nothing would occupy him. Those days I would call the other staff on the top floor and, if we needed to restrain him then insist that we do it on the floor in front of the surveillance cameras.

On one occasion we had to restrain him in the morning, because he was swinging at other patients and staff members. As usual, we were understaffed: only three workers, and everyone was awake.

Two of us restrained him and we asked the young woman who worked with us to keep calling school emergency numbers for backup and to oversee other students so they would not interfere in the restraining process. As we held him down, he somehow managed to move his right knee and hit my colleague, which opened a gash on his mouth and started bleeding. It was a chaotic scene, and my injured colleague wanted to withdraw but I begged him to hold on as it would have been dangerous to let him go at that moment. Another five minutes passed, and the patient calmed down.

The senior support staff arrived an hour later, checking that we had not hurt him during the restraining procedure. After ensuring the patient was safe, they turned to the injured staff member to get him an ambulance. As usual they consoled him that the school was going to pay his medical bills—as if this in itself was compensation.

As we sat on the couch waiting for the ambulance, he said, "Yasin, this is not worth it. I need to get out of here before I lose an eye for 12 bucks." I corrected him that it was actually less than that after they deducted the taxes, but I added that instead of frowning at the low pay in the dangerous workplace he should be frowning at his country's dictator, who has sold the nation to the lowest bidder and left its citizens wandering in the world. I told him the only kinds of jobs open for him as an immigrant were the 3 D's (Dirty, Demanding and Dangerous), and this was the case wherever he would go.

I wanted him to be thankful that the support staff had not found any marks on the boy to investigate us or even take us to court for abusing him. But still they had blamed us for restraining the boy with only the two of us, explaining it was not what they taught us. We realized they were trying to blame the young woman who had not joined in the restraint and we did stand up to say that we were at fault for asking her to stay away and take care of other students.

The young woman was in her early 20s, a daughter of immigrants from one of the neighboring U.S. islands, and in her first job while she pursued her college studies. A week earlier another patient had grabbed one of her breasts, squeezing it while she was administering his medications. She told him to stop and when we went to the ground floor level, we noticed the boy pleading to her for forgiveness. We asked her to write a report, but she decided against it because they wouldn't punish him because of his mental health disabilities.

Not all the misfortune was dealt to my colleagues; I had my fair share. One incident that really hurt me happened one morning when a patient was in the restroom for longer than usual—more than 20 minutes—and it was causing problems. When another student wanted to use the restroom, we had to redirect them either to the one in the basement or the one on the first floor.

This situation continued until it was time to board the vans and go to school, but the patient still hadn't come out. I knocked on the door, asking if he needed help or more time and there was no answer. Then I decided to open the door and there he was standing holding his own filth in his hands. When he saw me, he threw it in my face. We had to delay the trip to school for 30 minutes while we both cleaned up.

I considered myself lucky to have held onto this particular position for six months. I had seen many colleagues hired and fired.

I had even started picking up hours at the school, accompanying students and staying in class as a teaching assistant, helping them complete their class assignments, maintaining order, restraining a student when they turned violent in class, and taking them to gym. I would accompany them to the canteen, feeding lunch to those who needed help eating, and escorting students to the restroom and giving them any help they required there. For the four days I didn't work at my home health aide live-in job. I was working at the school during the day and at the group home at night. In total, I was working for this company 18 hours every day. The longer work hours also strained my effectiveness, especially at night when I had to stay awake. I was starting to read less and sleep more on the house sofas or chairs.

Like I said earlier, almost all the staff slept at some point during the night. But the night supervisors who came to check on that had once been residential staff members themselves and knew all the tricks.

Most night supervisors were Ugandans, and one in particular who was the Head of the Supervisor's Department was corrupt. He ran a racket in which he extorted money from the night staff in exchange for allowing them to sleep without being reported. I had heard about his racket but since he had not yet found me sleeping, he had not yet offered me a deal.

Inevitably on one of those busy days, he did indeed find me sleeping and demanded that I pay him $2,000 to keep the job. The amount was startling and I knew right away that I was not going to pay it but I sought to buy some time that day and I offered to pay him in four installments, starting from the next paycheck, which would come due in two days.

Other Ugandan people who also worked at the company told me his racket was an open secret, but the amount he sought to extort from me was excessive. Some told me he was extorting a lot because he knew I was working at the school and group home, which meant a lot of hours and in his understanding, I was making good money. Others told me that it was because I did not bargain that he always asked for large sums but with a bargain he would even take $500. I didn't see any reason to negotiate because I knew I was not going to give him any money.

Payday came and I ignored several of his calls. Then when I came back to work on Monday night, he found me sleeping on my computer laptop again and he said, "You don't want to pay but you want to sleep, I am not leaving until you pay the first installment here and now or you need to find another job."

I told him I had not been to the bank as I was running from job to another, but I suggested that we connect during the day. When I received his first missed call during the day, I knew it was time to call it off by reporting myself to the school management and resigning effectively. I told the house manager in a text message that he did not need to fire me as I was resigning because I could not pay the $2,000 the night supervisor wanted from me to cover up for my sleeping on duty at night. My resignation was accepted and upon investigating the supervisor's conduct, he was also fired.

I had built my life and career on investigating and reporting on corruption. I also realized how vulnerable I could become in such a situation, afraid that being honest would cost me the livelihood that I worked so hard to obtain.

Many migrant workers face the same predicament. The choice is particularly hard because doing the right thing offers little or no assurance of economic security. It is worth remembering that migrant workers make sacrifices that their critics would not countenance: there are reasons why few Americans take these jobs. Yet migrant workers ask for little more than a modicum of justice in terms of wage, working conditions, and prospects. Yet, one should think in good conscience what this hypocrisy means: when people demonize migrant workers who are trying desperately to do the right thing. There is a broader lesson of humility in the act of changing a soiled diaper for an elderly patient or for helping to calm a patient who does not know or understand why he acts violently. It is the gateway to human dignity and respect for everyone.

Can't You Read?
Driving Uber/Lyft

AFTER two years in the USA, I contemplated driving rideshare taxis for the companies Uber and Lyft. I desperately wanted to stop working at homes for people with disabilities, so instead I planned to drive for a living. That said, I decided to keep the PCA job with my quadriplegic client.

The plan sounds simple enough, but it didn't prove so. It is not as easy to enter the professional driving sector as it is to access others in the U.S. There are good reasons—in the form of employment restrictions—that keep caregiving as the only realistic option for new migrants.

One such restriction is that to drive for Uber you have to have an American driving permit that has been in use for at least a year; a stipulation that has kept many aspirant taxi drivers out of action for some time. By the time my license had been active for a year I had started saving for a new car that would help me to realize my plan, drive for Uber, and increase my income.

Another significant obstacle is that you must have a new car: the taxi companies only accept a car within a few years of its manufacture and many migrants, including me, had vehicles that are several years old.

So, my first challenge was to get a new car. My savings were still not adequate to pay for a vehicle that meets the requirements. I was still driving a 1999 Toyota Corolla that I had bought for $500 a few months after I arrived in the U.S., and though the ignition was good the body was falling apart. Friends used to tease me that I should drive carefully so as not to fall out through the holes in the door caused by the rust.

I talked with my brother Wahab about the difficulty of saving money in caregiving and his advice was to secure a car loan from the bank, but I was hesitant to start accumulating American debts before a decision about my asylum has been made.

One day I told him that I had found a good and affordable Honda Civic for sale—in a garage where I had my oil changed. My brother broke into laughter and said something to the effect that moving around garages and looking for a car to drive taxis on the road is like going to a hospital and asking nurses to hook you up with one of their longtime patients for marriage.

The large majority of Uber and Lyft drivers are immigrants. It's one of the easiest entry-level jobs to obtain in the U.S., and recruitment is handled online with minimal documentation required. I was surprised to learn that even the Employment Authorization Card—normally the first requirement for any job application, was not needed to apply to Uber or Lyft. Indeed, just four documents were: driver's license, car title, current inspection sticker, and vehicle insurance.

It came as a considerable relief to learn all this because not only was my employment authorization set to expire in a few months, but also the renewal process was taking as much time as for the asylum application. Without the authorization I would have lost the caregiving job—even if only temporarily—so I would at least be bringing in some income from driving.

Rideshare companies have often been criticized for not being more vigilant and rigorous in their recruiting, but these lapses are not so much the product of circumstance than as that of the companies trying to meet the demand for driving services. Again, as with so many other jobs, many American citizens shy away from these opportunities while immigrants are willing to be on the road as long as the demand for rides is there.

I want to step out of my personal narrative for a moment to look at the ridesharing sector in general, which has become a target in public discourse on immigration, one of the core tenets of which is the misguided belief that migrants are taking jobs from Americans. It is fair to say that Uber and Lyft may well qualify as emblematic of the wider gig economy, the benefits of which are not easy to discern, as any gig tends towards exploitation.

Uber drivers, who mostly work full time, are still classified legally as independent contractors, a status that doesn't obligate their employers to provide benefits, insurance coverage, or holiday pay.

Drivers have their own cars, purchase their own fuel, and keep up with car maintenance including oil changes, routine parts replacement and repairs for more serious problems, and cover the capital depreciation of the vehicle.

In short, the operational costs are passed to the owners of the cars and the profits to the owners of Uber. The only tool or material that Uber provides is the software and the digital infrastructure that facilitates ride transactions. In terms of actual pay: Uber decides what to pay drivers for each trip; a figure that fluctuates continuously depending on market and ride demands.

Furthermore, Uber claims it takes an average of 21 percent of earnings on each ride but in my personal experience it is—at least on occasion—the driver who ends up receiving the 21 percent.

Every completed trip registers the driver's earned compensation immediately. They might be dissatisfied with that amount but would have virtually no recourse to complaint and as a result receive a revised amount.

As drivers, we always call the feature of UberPool or shared rides for Lyft, a big rip-off. One time I took a pool from Boston to Peabody in Massachusetts and asked the passengers how much they had paid. Three paid Uber a total of $75 but Uber paid me just $26 for this trip.

Another reason drivers dislike these shared rides is because most customers using that service either have limited budgets or just refuse to tip.

This issue is about much more than rideshare companies. That a legally incorporated institution could get away with abuse on such a scale and still yield eye-watering profits sets a dangerous precedent within the corporate culture of the nation.

In addition, Uber has competed against small, franchised taxi businesses, forcing them to close. Again, some would prefer to blame immigrants for this. Uber and Lyft are cheap and accessible in many cities, and their convenience has lured customers into making the switch, as they no longer have to signal with their arms to catch a taxi or walk to a designated stand or station. Some people assumed that as taxi companies went out of business, their drivers would relent and join Uber or Lyft. It is akin to assuming that as legacy retailers have been forced out of the market, retail employees would take up jobs packing up boxes or delivering packages for e-tailer giants such as Amazon.

Many Americans forget that as these monopolies have emerged rapidly on the scene, the resulting income disparities are not because of immigrants taking jobs from them. It is easy for politicians to escape realities and fix blame on immigrants, while protecting the vested interests of corporate donors and lobbyists who are happy to fund political campaigns for such willing mouthpieces.

In its early years, Uber grew rapidly, as potential drivers were tantalized by the company's promising advertisements. Drivers could make up to $25 per hour, maintain a schedule tailored to their flexibility, and receive signing bonuses in the thousands of dollars.

In a survey of more than 2,600 active drivers with

calculations based on the Ridester's 2018 Independent Driver Earnings Survey, Uber's claims ring closer to the truth in some cities and are far from it in others.

Drivers in Honolulu, Long Island, and Seattle can earn the $25 per hour rate, as Uber claims. Meanwhile, in other major metropolitan areas around the country, drivers often earn an average of less than $10 per hour and below the federally mandated minimum hourly wage. This includes Akron, Ohio ($4.94 per hour) and Raleigh/Durham, North Carolina ($6.62 per hour). Some of the nation's largest cities fare just as poorly: Houston, for example, is just $8.72 per hour while Tampa-St. Petersburg in Florida is $8.95 per hour. Drivers spend more time on the road circling around and looking for riders and this time, fuel is not paid for or compensated. Uber does not even pay for fuel or time the driver takes to go and pick up a rider even though that may be some distance.

The drivers and their customers are separated by an economic divide that translates directly into geographical distance. They must live in cheap neighborhoods, a long way from the affluent areas that will generate fares. For example, I would have to drive 24 miles from Acton to Boston before I started picking up fares. Later, the distance grew as I commuted from Boxborough, some 30 miles away. It's not uncommon for Uber drivers in my area to sleep in their cars to minimize the cost of doing business.

The scale of the *commute* is not the only problem faced by drivers. To make any money they must work long hours, which makes staying awake and alert a challenge. Inevitably, some drivers push their limits. Uber has become aware of the problem, but it resolved it by automatically turning off the access to the mobile app once a driver has been online for 12 hours. However, most drivers will just switch over to Lyft.

To stay awake, drivers use coffee or caffeinated cold beverages. Now I understand the Dunkin' Donuts slogan: "America runs on Dunkin." It is an example of ironic truth in advertising.

But even the caffeine solution is not fail-safe. After drinking coffee bathroom, drivers need bathroom breaks so urgently that they have to give up requested trips, to locate an available nearby restroom. If the destination was the airport, finding a restroom would be easy enough. The challenge, though, was to rush in, use the facilities, and return to the car that was parked in the five-minute zone. Any delay would be costly, with a ticket issued by the airport police.

Destinations at a mall or shopping center are much more amenable for a quick rest stop but the worst were destinations in residential areas or Boston's central business district. I discussed these dilemmas with other Uber drivers, in the hopes of discovering a clever solution. One driver recommended to be looking always for a port-a-potty near a construction site or park with playground structures. He said construction managers often would allow him to use one, if he asked politely enough.

The most positive aspect of driving for Uber is finding a passenger with an interesting background story to tell. Some passengers make small talk about the weather or the city while others discuss politics, and yet others' conversations are of a more personal nature.

One memorable conversation was with a white female in her late twenties about her struggles to pay off her student loans. She told me the income from her teaching job could not sustain her financially and still make the debt obligations on a loan, so she had taken up a second job as a bartender for three days each week. She earned so much in tips from bartending that she wondered why the job that she went to college in order to get, could not provide enough.

"It's frustrating being there to serve and smile to happy people, when inside yourself you are not happy, but that smile is what brings the tips and from these tips I pay toward my student loan every month," she said.

I told her I shared her concerns and asked if she thought that immigrants were responsible for her financial problems. "*No,*" she replied. She blamed the government for not providing free college education and for not paying teachers well enough to live decently. I asked her whom she believed benefited the most from the student loan debt and she answered the corporate bankers. I then told her of how the same corporate banks had devastated economies in Africa and Latin America, with them contributing to the desperation that has forced immigrants to venture to the U.S. I added that those banks escape blame because they control politicians in Washington and have the means to influence the mainstream media narrative. As the trip concluded we had formed a bond, convinced we are both just victims of the same corporate greed.

Another memorable instance was a black American in his mid-twenties with his four-year-old son. The man told me he had been released from prison a week earlier and he was getting to know his son, who was born while he was incarcerated. He told me he was going to try as much as possible not to go back to prison because he wanted to stay with his son. He didn't want his son to grow up without a father's guidance because that could mean he might risk ending up in prison as he did. The man recalled that his own father had been arrested when he was young, and that his mother struggled to rear him and two siblings.

When they were teenagers, he recalled, they ended up on the streets to hustle and help their mother put food on the table. Having given up on school, he was arrested just before his 19th birthday. He didn't want to discuss his case, brushing aside my question with responses such as "usual stuff." But he told me that by the time he was arrested he had a girlfriend, whose father was also in jail, and that she was pregnant. When she visited him in jail, she promised him that she would not get an abortion but that she would hustle to earn enough money to take care of the baby. He added that few black families in America have grown up with fathers in the house; the white folks in police and courts have believed all black men belong in prisons and the cycle has been hard to break.

I asked him if he was trying to find a job and start working, and he told me he still was not having luck finding one because of the background checks that uncover criminal history and deem him unfit for employment. I could sense the strong bond between the son and father in their interactions in my car, even though they had just met. It was clear his son adored his father. Once they left, I only wondered how long the young man would be able to stay out of jail, without work, to be with his son.

Not all my interactions were positive. Some white clients did not hide their racist attitudes.

One white man asked me for a favor before he sat in my car. He had locked his car keys inside, and he said if I could help him open his car and get his keys, he would pay me the Uber fare without needing me to take him to his destination.

His explanation was unclear at first, and I tried to repeat the details back to him. I asked if he wanted me to break into his car and retrieve his keys and he said that was the request. I understood that this was a favor he would only ask from a black driver. I told him I didn't know how to break into a car; that even if my own car was locked, I would be unable to do so. He sat in my vehicle, visibly distraught because I had let him down.

Clients also bring their daily experiences and moods into an Uber trip. One day, a woman who appeared to be middle age, entered my car and announced as I started the engine that she was pregnant and if I hit any potholes with such force that she could have a miscarriage, she would sue me and Uber. After arriving at her destination, I asked her if she was fine and the baby was still intact, she said yes, and I breathed a sigh of relief.

Another time, I picked up an old couple in their mid-seventies at a Boston hospital and the wife told me they had had a bad day: her husband Jack had just been diagnosed with cancer. She told me the doctors were willing to help but they also asked for the husband's cooperation, which meant quitting his smoking habit—something he hesitated to do.

"Imagine: when I went to do the paperwork after that bad news, I came back to where I left Jack and he was missing," the woman said. "I looked for him everywhere and couldn't find him. Then I went where people smoke and there he was, smoking again."

I decided to offer my own encouragement, telling Jack it was better for him to quit smoking and that the doctors had the ability to give him a longer life if he quit smoking. Jack had not said a word since he entered my car but then he blurted, "If you two don't stop picking on me, I am stopping this Uber right here and giving you a single-star rating with a nasty comment." I apologized and stayed quiet for the remainder of the trip.

It was his wife who continued talking: "Jack, you are threatening a poor Uber driver for telling you something that is good. Jack, that is not right. Please, Jack, say sorry to him." After we arrived at their destination, I checked my app and Jack had given me a $5 tip.

Green Card Brides

AFTER she'd kissed her two small boys good-bye at the Entebbe International Airport, Susan Namutebi forced herself to walk away from them despite hearing the screams from her baby, only six months old and still breastfeeding. Susan struggled to maintain her composure as her mother held onto the children. If she broke down and wept at the airport, the security guards might arrest her, suspecting her of trafficking drugs or some other crime.

The reality was that she was leaving Uganda not to commit a crime, but because she had no other choice.

Susan was a high school history and economics teacher in Uganda. She had met her husband David Sebatta, a fellow teacher, at the school where she worked in the Mubende District of western Uganda. Their modest joint income made it possible for them to buy a small plot of land and build a house. They were struggling but happy.

Then the government grabbed their land.

"Our evictions were announced on community radios, and promises of compensation were made that were never followed," Susan told me in Boston.

Her story about government corruption should have shocked me, but since we're from the same country and I've investigated the issue of land grabbing by the Ugandan government, it did not. I'd heard this story too many times before.

*

In July 2015, a colleague from the Thomson Reuters news agency contacted me for help in translating and transcribing the interviews she'd conducted in southern Uganda with some of the 14,000 villagers evicted from their land when the Ugandan government leased 8,000 hectares to Green Resources, a Norwegian timber company, in the forested area of Bukaleba. The villagers complained that they no longer had rights to the land on which they were born and had farmed for generations.

This was a flagrant case of land-grabbing, but what

struck me most about the interviews I translated was that the villagers detailed the direct involvement of President Yoweri Kaguta Museveni himself. Museveni had written a letter promising them 500 hectares elsewhere in Uganda in exchange for their willingness to relocate. But the land was not demarcated, and there was an endless debate about where, exactly, this land was and who had a right to use it.

The chairman of the Bukaleba village said that the Norwegian company had lied and had planted trees on the land set aside for the evicted villagers. As of this writing, the villagers have been waiting for years for the Ugandan government to allocate the 500 hectares to them as agreed.

The story of these villagers is symbolic of the disenfranchised African's position between the rock of Corruption and the hard place of Nepotism. These villagers—who number in the thousands—were rendered homeless by a deal done above their heads and behind their backs between Ugandan and European elites.

Land grabbing is one of the biggest reasons why people are fleeing Africa for what they perceive as better lives in Europe, America, or the Middle East. Meanwhile, the policy makers in those places insist on blocking their legal entry and right to work. Let's look at how Susan's life has unfolded to put a human face on this particular immigration crisis.

*

Susan—and David were forced to leave Uganda after they lost their land and home to the New Forests Company (NFC) in 2010, after the UK-based company made a deal with the Ugandan government to plant and harvest timber. When it became clear that the promised compensation was not forthcoming, Susan and David filed a lawsuit against the Ugandan government and began showing up in court.

What happens in these cases is that the people who are educated enough and courageous enough to go to court are often assassinated. Soon, David began receiving threats against his life, and it became apparent that the only hope he and Susan had for a better future was to leave Uganda.

Both of them wanted to come to the United States. When David applied for a visa to the U.S., however, his application was denied. He managed to go to Dubai with a loan from family members, and once he got there, he found work in hotel security. He used his salary to pay for Susan's immigration to the U.S. with the help of a man in Kampala who helped prepare her for the immigration interview and booked her plane ticket—all at great expense.

Susan tearfully left her young sons Simone and

Samson in the care of her mother and sisters. Now, after a few years, Susan's youngest son is old enough to beg her to come home.

"Mum, do you have a car?" her little son asked once.

"Yes," Susan replied.

"Then drive the car and come home!" the boy pleaded.

Susan cried all night.

She had filed for asylum when she arrived in the U.S. in 2015 on the basis of persecution, claiming she had been violently evicted from their land by a European corporation with the help of the Ugandan government and her life had been threatened. Unfortunately, she had no proof of the threats against her life, and people are constantly fleeing economic deprivation all over the world. There's no asylum category for poverty.

In addition, the backlog in processing asylum claims in the U.S. was so enormous that Susan finally decided to try getting a Green Card through an arranged marriage. That way, she could at least visit Uganda again and see her children without fear of being denied re-entry into the U.S., where she'd found work as a caregiver in three different residential institutions for teenagers with disabilities.

With her husband's encouragement, Susan applied

for a divorce so that she could remarry, this time to a U.S. citizen. However, getting divorced was easy compared to finding an American citizen willing to enter into a false marriage with her.

Susan talked to several men with citizenship who were in the market to sell their papers, and finally settled on a man I'll call "Timothy Walusimbi" because he was the son of her father's best friend. Timothy assured Susan that a deal with him would be expensive, but better than a deal with any other man because he wouldn't demand sex from her in the process.

"Our fathers are friends, so you're like a sister to me," Timothy said.

That assurance was important to Susan who, for the five years she had already been in the U.S., had consistently reassured her husband that he was the only man in her life.

Timothy's fee to marry her was $30,000; he asked Susan to pay half of it to start the process. "You can pay me the balance in monthly installments of $1500," he said, "with full payment due by the time we go for an immigration interview."

In addition, Timothy expected Susan to pay any related costs, like the fee for the marriage certificate and an immigration lawyer. The lawyer's fee was $4000; Susan paid $2000 up front and the remainder in monthly installments of $500. She worked three jobs, with a total of more than 100 hours a week, but she couldn't accrue any savings because she was barely funding her Green Card. Still, Susan was hopeful that it would all work out, and that one day she'd be reunited with her husband and children in the U.S.

Then Timothy balked when it was time to sign the lawyer's papers to give his consent to representation. "Just copy my signature on the papers," he said. "I'm too busy to meet you and sign the papers in person."

Susan was furious—and panicked. By then, she had already paid Timothy more than $20,000. If Timothy couldn't make himself available simply to sign a paper, was he going to be available to go to the lawyer's preparatory meetings and the immigration interview? What if there were more immigration interviews that required him to be present? What if she lost all of this money to him and the marriage didn't go through?

She knew that these "marriages" depended almost entirely on the goodwill of the person with citizenship. If Timothy pulled out of the process after collecting the money, she would have no legal recourse. In desperation, Susan contacted her father and asked him to speak with his friend, Timothy's father. "I need you to encourage him to take the process seriously," Susan begged.

Somehow, her father and Timothy's dad managed to talk Timothy into cooperating, and he finally showed up to sign the lawyer's papers.

Not long after that, Susan was hit at her workplace by one of the clients she was caring for, a boy with intellectual challenges. The boy pushed her down a staircase, and as she rolled down the stairs, she broke her arm. She was put on a two months' leave with a 75% salary.

This was generous, she knew, but it was still only compensation from one job, and now she couldn't work her other two. How could she possibly keep up the payments to Timothy?

Timothy refused to accept any delays. "Hey, you're going to have to make a choice between nursing your broken arm or paying for your Green Card," he said. "I'm not waiting for my money."

Susan was trapped. She asked her doctor to reduce her sick leave to just one month so that she could return to work, but the doctor refused her pleas, insisting that her arm needed time to heal. She had no choice but to hand over almost all of her monthly compensation for the injury to Timothy for the months she never worked.

*

Land grabs in Africa are just one iteration of the paradoxical relationship between the continents: European and American corporations are evicting Africans from their own land to pave the way for profitable agriculture projects, while at the same time those governments are preventing displaced people from migrating to their countries.

Bukaleba's villagers are among millions facing an uncertain future across Africa where, according to a report by the U.S.-based Oakland Institute, an estimated 50 million hectares of land have been leased to foreign entities and 90 percent of rural land remains untitled.

Land is both the only form of property and source of stable income for most African families. Taking it way means that people across the continent have nothing. Yet, across Africa, dictators are rushing to introduce land reforms designed to take land away from citizens in exchange for quick cash from foreign investors. Displaced Africans only hope leave their countries and migrate to places where there is at least some hope of finding work so they can feed their families.

In Ethiopia, for example, thousands of people from the Anuak Gambella region fled the country as the government launched a program in which whole communities were forcibly resettled. The Ethiopian government used threats, violence, and powers of arrest against those who resisted in order to sell fertile land to foreign investors. According to the Oakland

Institute, at least 3,619,509 hectares of land in Ethiopia have been transferred to investors. Most of the people who were relocated had limited access to food or farming afterward, and some starved.

In another graphic example, in 2008 South Korean conglomerate Daewoo announced it was leasing 1.3 million hectares (3.2 million acres) of Madagascar for 99 years for about $12 an acre—a small fraction of the cost of farmland in the Republic of South Korea (RSK) —to grow maize. The maize would then be harvested for ethanol production in RSK. That amounts to half of Madagascar's arable land and is among the largest land lease deals in postcolonial Africa. Meanwhile, Madagascar ranks as one of the poorest countries in the world; its citizens must frequently rely on the World Food Program (WFP) to save them from malnutrition and starvation.

This land deal fueled popular anger and led to the overthrow of then Madagascar President Marc Ravalomanana in 2009. His successor, Andry Rajoelina, canceled the deal ahead of his inauguration, saying, "We are not against the idea of working with investors, but if we want to sell or rent out land, we have to change the constitution; you have to consult the people."

Many Western investors, including Wall Street bankers and wealthy individuals, have turned their attention to agricultural land acquisition in Africa. This shift places the food system in Africa in the hands of a few Western corporations whose interests are, first and foremost, economic gain, not feeding the world's hungry.

The American investor Philippe Heilberg signed a farmland deal with Paulino Matip, a Sudanese warlord, to lease 400,000 hectares of land (an area the size of Dubai) in South Sudan in July 2008 (the deal wasn't reported until January 2009.) That same year, Heilberg increased his acreage by 800,000 additional hectares. Heilberg was open about his belief that several African states were likely to break apart in the coming years, and that the political and legal risks he took would be amply rewarded.

"If you bet right on the shifting of sovereignty then you are on the ground floor," he said.

Four years later, Heilberg, a self-described libertarian who is also referred to as a "cowboy capitalist," had second thoughts about his gambit. As Vice media reported, "There is no governance; it's a complete, utter disaster," Heilberg said about his dealings in South Sudan in a speech to Duke University students. "Until ministers found to be corrupt are hanged or severely punished, it won't be stopped."

Western corporations haven't been the only players in a new race to acquire fertile African land and displace Africans. Asia and the Gulf Middle East were also aggressive in acquiring large chunks of African land to stabilize food supply in their own countries, thereby averting domestic social unrest and political instability. The only problem is that the political stability in their countries was acquired at the expense of Africans, whose corrupt governments do not prioritize domestic food supply or local production over foreign investment and production for export.

Qatar, with only one percent of its land suitable for farming, has purchased 40,000 hectares for $3.4 billion in Kenya to grow crops. Al Qudra, an Abu Dhabi-based investment company, also bought large tracts of farmland in Morocco and Algeria. Today the Gulf Middle East countries are among key destinations for African migrants who've been robbed of their land and other possessions in Africa.

While of course it's important to invest in the African agricultural sector, the West's acquisition of continental land is a threat to African economies and livelihoods. These land deals often lack transparency and are frequently mismanaged by governments. Smallholder farmers are the ones typically being displaced in the process, and with no other livelihood possible, they are resorting to migration.

It is profoundly sad for the government or the president of an African country to be facilitating the ownership of land to foreigners. This is direct exploitation. Citizens don't even have ownership of land in their own country.

While African nations have tried to institute land administration reforms with varying degrees of success, critical challenges remain. The area formally recognized under statutory law is much less than the area to which Indigenous Peoples and local communities hold customary rights. Further action is needed to bridge that gap.

In many countries, laws may recognize community control, but need to be strengthened to recognize more robust rights of ownership. Even where ownership is recognized, laws or regulations may limit certain uses of the land, particularly for commercial purposes. Incompatible laws governing other sectors — like extractive industries, agribusiness, and conservation — can also adversely impact indigenous and community land rights.

Moreover, formal legal recognition of indigenous and community lands do not guarantee tenure security. States and other actors must also respect, support, and enforce such legal protections.

In Africa, European and American foreigners own the land, mines, banks, factories, fuel stations, and airlines. All of the wealth coming from these sources is being shipped or transferred to the West. There is nothing left in Africa for Africans, and citizens of these countries cannot stay home. Like Susan and her husband, many have no choice but to migrate.

In 2017, the Ugandan government tabled a land bill amendment proposal on compulsory acquisition of land for public use. President Museveni explained to Uganda's citizens that the amendment is framed for the country's better interests, and tried to convince the public that having the government take over land from farmers they deem "unsuitable" for agriculture and giving it to investors will ultimately bring in more revenue.

African leaders often designate farmland as "public" so they can then sell it. The African leaders who are handing over fertile African land to Western corporations are doing the same thing that colonialists did in earlier times when they designated millions of acres as public land. In Kenya, after the highlands were declared "crown land," the British colonialists handed 100,000 acres over to Lord Delamere for a penny per acre. Lord Francis Scott purchased 350,000 acres and the East African Syndicate Ltd. took 100,000 acres, all at giveaway prices.

In Liberia in 1926, the Firestone Rubber Company acquired a million acres of forest land at a cost of six cents per acre. In the Congo, King Leopold II issued decrees that designated all free parcels as government land— in effect, as his own property. He amassed all of the parcels that the natives hadn't cultivated and set those aside as hunting grounds, a plentiful source of wood to build with, or for mining iron ore to be used in tools and weapons. The 21st century has seen that practice continue, albeit in a different form.

The exploitation of African people, especially poor, uneducated farmers, is being exacerbated by long-ruling Western puppets like Uganda's Museveni. This practice continues to negatively impact the continent's future. African resources are fast becoming depleted and outpaced by population growth. By 2050, the population in most African countries will have doubled, and the continent will have depleted nearly all of its resources. As a result, more African migrants will continue trying to get to Europe or the U.S.—countries where African resources have built stable economies.

Europe and the U.S. are already concerned about these demographics, especially since the family planning strategies the West has promoted in Africa haven't worked. Visa restrictions and border patrols are likely to be tightened, but no restrictions are rigorous enough to stop the wave of migrations.

*

After many months, Susan submitted her application to have her marriage approved. Now she needed to finish paying all of Timothy's installments somehow and prepare for her immigration interviews. She also had to put some of her clothes into Timothy's apartment in case the immigration officials paid them a surprise visit. She'd been told by their lawyer that she and Timothy would likely be subjected to a visit at the apartment by immigration officials whose job it was to ascertain if they truly lived together.

Susan felt fine about bringing her dresses over there, but what about her bras and panties? She hated the idea of Timothy having them and considered buying a few new things to put in his apartment. But what if an immigration officer actually visited and went through her things? Surely it would look strange if all of her clothes were new. Guiltily, she took some of her used undergarments over to Timothy's place and left them there.

She and Timothy also had to prepare for the likely immigration questions. The preparations would help them give similar answers to the same questions in case they were interviewed separately. For instance, one of the most common questions, according to other migrant workers Susan knew, was which side of the bed your husband or wife sleeps on. The questions could get explicit, too, regarding sexual activities. While rehearsing the trial interview questions, they had to be equally explicit about the types and colors of underwear and intimate apparel they wore. This was because the interviewer might ask, "Did you see your wife dress up this morning? Tell us what she is wearing?"

The preparations for Susan and Timothy Greencard's marriage interview were grueling, but most frustrating was that even though she had already paid Timothy all his dues, he practically demanded extra for everything else they were doing. He would sometimes refuse to show up at the lawyer's office, insisting that she pay him to be present. Susan always obliged because, at this point, Timothy had nothing to lose. The burden was entirely on her; risking loss of her $30,000 investment and the possibility of never being eligible for a green card if this arrangement did not work.

On the day of the interview, she practically had to bribe him to attend. Fortunately, she received her green card on the first interview, confirming her belief that marriage-based green cards represented the easiest path to U.S. citizenship. The initial green card, however, was valid for only two years. After that, she would face another hurdle: renewing it for ten years, which meant cozying up again to Timothy, her fake husband.

At the moment, Susan decided not to worry about the renewal. Instead, she planned to visit Uganda and see her sons and her legal husband Michael. She also had to purchase a ticket for Michael, who was working in Dubai, to join them in Uganda for a family reunion. The couple would be reunited with their kids for a month.

Susan said she could not find the words to describe her first encounter with her youngest son, Samson. He was so adorable. Now four years old, he had grown into a curious boy with endless questions and solutions. For example, he often repeated the questions he asked his mom on the phone, such as whether she had a car in America and why she didn't often drive home.

"Oh, sweetie, I would love to do that, but you know from America to Uganda there are big lakes and oceans. A car cannot cross the oceans unless you want your mama to die." He shook his head, indicating he didn't like hearing about such a prospect.

The next day, out of nowhere, he brought up the same conversation. "Mama," he called.

"Yes, sweetie," Susan replied.

"I have an idea."

"Okay, tell me."

"Mama, you can buy a car that turns into a boat when it gets to the sea and sail through the ocean.

Then it gets to the water and turns into a car, and you come to Uganda."

Susan knew her son watched a lot of cartoons to get such ideas, but still, the idea moved her to tears. Seeing her son trying so hard to fix her life, stretching his young brain to solve all the family problems, touched her.

"We always had to chase him every night from our bedroom to go to his bed. It was like he was afraid if he let us alone, we might sneak out and go back to America." In the morning, the first thing he always asked when he woke up was, "Is Mum still here?" His first destination was always their bedroom, but his dad would ask him to first use the bathroom and brush his teeth. Still, in no time, he would be back. He wanted to be with his mum the entire time and had so many questions about why they were separated.

"Mum, why don't you want to take me to America with you?"

"I will take you one day," Susan promised.

"Mum, if I go with you to America, I will behave myself. I will not fight with Simone. And if snow falls, I will eat all the snow on your car. You won't have to plow it."

Susan noticed that Samson seemed to be much closer to her than to his dad, possibly because Michael returned home every year, while Susan had been away for over three years. Having left when Samson was about six months old, it felt like he was meeting his mum for the first time.

The holiday passed quickly, and the 33 days flew like seconds on a clock. Susan worried about how to say good-bye to her two sons. They decided to leave at night while Samson was asleep, without saying good-bye. He would find out in the morning that his mum had left, but their dad would stay with them for an extra week.

After returning from Uganda, Susan and Timothy's relationship became even more parasitic. Timothy devised new ways to extort money from her every day. He demanded that in order to file taxes together as a married couple, he should be the sole beneficiary of the refunds. In total, he demanded $5,000 every year they filed jointly, and whenever the refunds fell short of that amount, Susan had to cover the balance from her pocket.

The tax money was not enough to satisfy Timothy. He treated Susan like an ATM, demanding money from her without any reason whenever he was broke. He told her to consider him as her employee in this transaction, working for her benefit. He insisted that it was in her best interests to keep him happy if she wanted to secure her citizenship. Every time they had to meet their lawyer or join a Zoom call, he asked for what he called a "per diem." Every time he called, he wanted money, and he called quite often. Whenever she saw his phone call, she panicked, and her blood pressure rose. She couldn't sleep without taking multiple sleeping pills.

Timothy would demand that she deposit $1,000 into the joint account they had set up to prove they were staying together and sharing bills. These calls were often followed by threats like, "If you don't give me that money, don't ask me for anything regarding renewing your Green Card."

His requests to extort more money fell outside their original agreement, especially when Susan already had paid the agreed-upon amount before the first interview. She often felt helpless and gave into his demands. Timothy's relentless tactics worked because she was so desperate and vulnerable that she could be manipulated with just a few threatening words and would send him more money without delay.

The two years moved quickly and it was time for Susan to switch out her conditional green card for a permanent one, which she could renew every ten years, as U.S. citizens do with their passports. Predictably, Timothy demanded more money. He wanted $5,000 to sign her renewal application as her husband. This time, Susan had to take out a personal loan from the bank to pay him.

After filing for the renewal, immigration backlogs delayed the process, and the new green card was not forthcoming. Meanwhile, Timothy continued to demand money from her. Most of Susan's income went towards paying rent and satisfying Timothy's financial demands. She calculated that she had paid him up to $75,000 since their deal began.

"When he first told me why he wanted $30,000—an exaggerated amount according to the green card market—he explained that he wanted to go through nursing school and that the money I gave him would pay for tuition and help with upkeep. It all sounded reasonable because I wanted him to gain something tangible from the transaction," Susan explained. "But now he has graduated after I paid all his tuition, and instead of saying 'thank you,' he has turned into a monster that cares about nothing but my money—all of it."

"I can't muster the courage to tell him to stop asking me for more money because I'm afraid everything I have paid for until now will unravel," she said. "If he walks away while I'm still on a conditional green card, there's no court I can take him to. I feel angry at myself for being so weak. How could I allow all this abuse for so long?"

The USCIS backlogs added to the tension. Every time Susan told Timothy she was broke or hadn't been paid yet, he would yell into the phone that he wanted nothing more to do with the arrangement. He blamed the delays at USCIS on Susan and threatened to walk away before the renewal. He claimed he wanted a divorce because he now wanted to marry a real generous wife who would support him financially, not a fake stingy one. He said it was Susan's problem that the process hadn't gone as quickly as it should have.

Susan panicked. If they divorced at this stage, she would lose everything without gaining the citizenship they had agreed upon initially. She understood that Timothy was likely faking his desire for a divorce to extort more money, but she was too afraid to confront him.

Desperate, Susan hoped that her parents might intervene. However, she soon realized that even their parents, who had earlier helped persuade Timothy to be more reasonable, were no longer helpful. Timothy no longer answered her father's calls, and Timothy's father, Fred, sided with his son, telling Susan to comply with whatever Timothy demanded.

Timothy kept his promise not to ask her for sex, but his extortion and blackmail for money made her feel just as violated, exhausted, and tired. The sad reality was that she didn't see any quick exit. The green card renewal process seemed endless. She thought that if she got the ten-year green card, she could divorce Timothy because there was a provision for gaining citizenship as a divorcee.

The rules were clear: if a marriage ended while the individual was still on a conditional green card, the chances of being naturalized would be affected, and the person could be deported. But if the marriage ended while holding a permanent green card, then the divorce wouldn't affect the individual's chances for becoming naturalized.

Timothy once called Susan while she was in the hospital, recovering from surgery for fibroids. Despite knowing she was in the hospital, he still demanded money. "When we made this deal, we didn't consider there would be backlogs and delays for green card renewals. You are going to give me another $5,000 for every extra year we wait for your renewal. Once the renewal comes, we immediately divorce. When can you give me the $5,000 for this year?"

The $5,000 demand was Timothy's constant refrain. Susan remained silent on the phone for about a minute, her mouth open in disbelief. A friend, Sheila Nalweyiso, who was taking care of her in the hospital and was familiar with the Timothy ordeal, asked for the phone to respond on her behalf, but Susan waved her down. In a faint, pleading voice, she told him, "You know I'm in the hospital. I don't have money."

"I didn't say give me the money now. I said, "When can you give me the money?" Timothy replied, his voice raised to clarify his intent.

"I don't know, Timothy. I'm in the hospital."

"If you don't want to give me the money, consider the deal null and void. I will not be calling you again," he said, adding, "From today, you will not be receiving any letters from my address until you pay."

By now, Sheila was wrestling Susan to take the phone out of her hand, and when she finally got it, she went to the phonebook, clicked on Timothy's number, and blocked it. Susan didn't know what Sheila had done when she handed the phone back.

Likely, Timothy unsuccessfully called multiple times that day, If he wanted money, he would call non-stop until he got it or received a promise that it was coming.

The following day, Timothy's sister Joanne called Susan. Her initial instinct was she was calling to sympathize with Susan for being in the hospital, but that was not the case. Joanne was calling to complain about Susan not answering her brother's calls. She threatened that Susan had no right to refuse Timothy's demands for money if she still wanted a permanent green card or citizenship.

"You can just go to the bank, get a loan of $5,000, and pay the bank in installments," Joanne advised.

It now appeared to Susan that extorting money from her had become a family business, and the whole family was out to make her feel bad for standing up for herself.

"You either give him the money, or you pay for your divorce and start all over."

"And what happens if I don't do either of the two?" Susan asked.

"Timothy is a citizen. He can still ask for a divorce and have the lawyers serve you. Then you will also pay him damages. You will have to pay double on your deportation day."

When Sheila visited Susan that evening to see how she was coping, she told her about Joanne's call, which infuriated Sheila. She waited until Susan was scrolling through her phone, then took it from her hands. Sheila insisted she wanted to have a word with Joanne, a woman-to-woman talk if she couldn't talk to Timothy, but Susan was still terrified of anyone intervening on her behalf.

"If Timothy has his family supporting his extortion, then someone should defend you, Susan. Come on," she pleaded. Sheila stormed out of the apartment with Susan's phone. Outside, she decided not to pick a fight with Joanne; she simply blocked her too. Then she clicked on Timothy's number, which was still blocked. She wrote a short message to Timothy without unblocking him:

"Timothy, if you want to file for divorce, I will file a fraud complaint for you stealing a total of $75,000 in a green card marriage scam. I have all the evidence of payments. If you think I'm stupid, you're wrong. I'm already talking to others who have been through similar ordeals."

She pressed send and then deleted the message. She brought the phone back to Susan and didn't tell her about the message. When Susan asked what she had told Joanne, Sheila lied and said Joanne had agreed to stay out of it.

It was only a week later that Sheila revealed what she had done to defend her. Susan, in a panic, unblocked both her tormentors but hesitated when she wanted to call them. She waited for another few weeks, but no one called her. Then she called them to apologize, as cowardly as she felt. Still, none of them mentioned divorce again. About five months later, Susan received her permanent green card, and they filed for divorce. She knew Sheila had helped her immensely by standing up to her bullies and thanked her.

Two years after the divorce, Susan applied for citizenship as a divorcee and it was granted. She was also able to bring her sons, Simone and Samson, to the

U.S. She still relives the harrowing memories of her green card ordeal but she is grateful that she finally found a happy ending.

*

When it was finally time for her immigration interview at the Mexican-U.S. border, Margaret, another Ugandan migrant, clung to her three-week-old daughter. She'd arrived at the border a month ago and had given birth to the girl in the Mexican camp for refugees. She was still sore and exhausted.

While the officials asked Margaret questions, the baby fussed occasionally, but was quickly quieted when Margaret rocked her.

One of the immigration officers asked to have a closer look at the baby. Instead of saying "she's so cute" or any of the usual pleasant remarks people made about the baby, the officer said, "She looks so white. Are you sure you're the baby's mother?"

Margaret took a deep breath. She knew this time would come, and she'd been trying to prepare for it. Still, it was difficult to tell the story of how she, a black woman from Uganda, had conceived a white baby girl en route to the USA.

Margaret had graduated with a bachelor's degree in social sciences from Makerere University. She was working as a hotel receptionist, collecting $85 dollars a month, when she got married and had her first child, a little boy. That's when the reality of the economic conditions in Uganda hit her. She tried to find a better paying job, but there was nothing. Unemployment rates were skyrocketing and the only certain future was poverty.

Her only hope was to migrate to the U.S. Her journey with other prospective migrants involved multiple stopovers in different countries. From Uganda she moved to Kenya, then to Brazil, where Margaret was grouped with seven other African migrants from Uganda, Congo, Cameroon, and Kenya. For a time, the group was stranded in Brazil when the trafficker told them he could no longer help them travel, since President Trump had changed the rules of entry for immigrants.

Margaret and her fellow African migrants desperately began hunting for other traffickers who would take them to the U.S. Meanwhile, they needed more money to live on, since the previous trafficker who had brought them from Africa didn't refund any of the enormous sums they'd paid him, and they weren't allowed to work in Brazil.

Margaret kept calling her husband and other relatives for financial help, but there was little they could send. Two of her friends managed to raise money from family in Uganda and paid a white man to take them to the Mexican border, where they knew they'd have to surrender themselves to the immigration officials. Their only avenue for entering the U.S. legally was to apply for asylum at the border.

In desperation, Margaret approached the white man and begged him to take her to the border as well. "I'll pay you back when I find a job in the U.S.," she said, but the trafficker agreed to take her only if she slept with him.

The trafficker refused to use a condom during sex, and a few weeks after she arrived in Mexico in the refugee camp, Margaret did a pregnancy test and it came out positive. She had a lot of mixed thoughts on the pregnancy, but she didn't believe in abortion and hoped the baby would bring her closer to the U.S.

Margaret finally managed to make it to the U.S. when President Biden took office and eased some of the restrictions at the U.S. Mexican Border. She is currently staying with friends in Boston, where she has to wear an electronic monitoring device (GPS ankle monitor) on her right leg until her court case is decided.

*

Arranged marriages are an easier path to American citizenship than applying for asylum.

Many African immigrants would rather pay to get married than go through the hassle of finding documents as evidence for the asylum process and then waiting years for it to be completed.

Still, even these marriages have their challenges. The putative spouses demand large sums, and documentation indicating shared accommodation and utility bills proving that the two are cohabiting as a married couple, sometimes becomes difficult to compile because immigration officials could easily verify their authenticity or lack thereof—a discovery that would lead to serious consequences.

There is also a performance required at the relevant meetings. The couple have to turn up holding hands, looking in one another's eyes and willing to display the appropriate gestures of affection.

In a shared house I stayed in when I arrived in America, there was an African woman in her fifties, renting one of the rooms in the house because she was having trouble with her arranged spouse, an African-American citizen.

She had paid $10,000 in installments to this man for the fake marriage and, after she completed the payments, the man demanded sexual intercourse.

Frequently, they would meet in the living room of

the boarding house before going to the immigration meetings, and the rest of us could hear them arguing.

The man told the woman that it was the last time he was going to the meetings and having to put on a show of fake smiles and kisses if she didn't let him into her bed.

And, the woman would retort, in a pleading tone, reminding him she had paid all the money he asked for and sex was not part of the package. She had a son almost his age, and she told him that she could not agree to his request. Achieving the American Dream through fake marriage is an expensive exercise that costs not only a lot of money but also a person's dignity.

Being Black in America

MANY images, including video footage of a Minneapolis police killing of George Floyd and scenes of African immigrants sleeping on the streets of Guangzhou in China, after being evicted during a racist fallout in which they were accused of spreading the COVID-19 virus, have unleashed an intense outpouring of emotions in Black people all around the world.

Between 2014 and 2020, police in the U.S. killed over 6,500 people. About 25 percent of those killed by the police were Black, even though Black people in the U.S. make up only 13 percent of the over-all population. As Black Lives Matter protests have mushroomed across all over U.S. states and at least 18 countries, the gatherings have emphasized that Black lives from all perspectives must be included in the dialogue, including those of African immigrants. It was more than 20 years ago, for example, when Amadou Diallo, 22, from Guinea, was shot and killed by four New York City police officers. They later claimed to mistake the victim for a suspect in a rape case. Diallo, who had no criminal record, was unarmed. The officers, who later were found not guilty, fired 41 shots, 19 of which struck the young immigrant in the February 1999 incident. In 2004, Diallo's family received a $3 million settlement under New York's wrongful death statute.

Black people of African ancestry continue to be viewed suspiciously throughout the world. In China, photos showing printed signs banning black people from entering shops to buy food have been shared widely across social media. Meanwhile, the Chinese government has denied any racist sentiments were behind the actions.

The attacks on Black people are not new. For instance, African migrants have been murdered in the Middle East, and Europeans have done little to save African migrants from drowning in makeshift boats as they seek refuge in their countries. And, in the U.S., innocent Black citizens continue to be gunned down indiscriminately by the police or self-proclaimed white nationalists or vigilantes. The abuse and torture of Black people is happening around the world. What can we do to stop it? What does the future hold for ordinary Black people? What does it mean to be Black in a world where hate is on the rise? What will happen to our children and grandchildren? These questions ring more acutely now as the Covid-19 pandemic's most serious effects are being felt everywhere.

This present moment is absolutely the right time to deal with these questions, especially as the public health crisis has exposed so many disparities and inequalities in historically disadvantaged communities. Sadly, it is not only Europeans or Americans citizens who not yet ready for a honest debate about the reasons behind African migrations. Even my fellow Africans are unprepared, afraid, or paralyzed to address the metaphorical elephant in the room.

We cannot afford to bury these injustices and go on because the risks of having our children and grandchildren living on this planet as second-class citizens pleading desperately with Europeans, Americans, or the Chinese to just take them on, even if it means being subservient to the point of slavery, have become inexcusable and unacceptable. The pandemic has revealed a crisis of human dignity on many dimensions. The plight of Africans is just one of them.

The Black Lives Matter protests are unlike previous events. The anger against police is being fused with the frustrations of economic inequities that have only been exacerbated by the corporate practices of global capitalism. As we struggle and eventually find our way to a new normal, there is the political will to rectify many long-standing injustices. One should involve a thorough, honest discussion about the future of 'Blackness' on this planet. We should not expect to find answers in summits led and orchestrated mainly by Americans and Europeans. After all, we should never trust the arsonists to be firefighters.

The migrant crisis and the American response to it is entirely consistent with a history of racist violence toward the indigenous population, slaves, and immigrants. Too many people still ask why people continue risking everything to take dangerous, desperate journeys to other countries illegally. Why can't they just do it the "right way" and arrive legally?

Because we have no choice but to leave our countries. Black people in American need to work with us and not against us, because they will never be respected as equal until Africa, their motherland, is respected.

We all dream of a place where we are equal to all. Does such a place exist?

*

Black migrants in the U.S. are subject to the same systemic racism as Black Americans. For instance, not long ago, I was waiting for a passenger in front of South Station. As an Uber driver, you receive an exact address on your phone that tells you where to meet someone, and that's where I parked. As I was waiting, a policeman came up and rapped angrily on the window with his knuckles. I rolled the window down, wondering what I'd done wrong.

"Can't you even read?" he shouted, gesturing angrily at a sign I hadn't seen that indicated I was waiting in a bus stop. "There's no parking here!"

"I'm not parked here," I explained. "I'm an Uber driver, and my passenger gave me this address."

"Yes, that's my fault, I'm sorry!" A breathless young white guy was climbing into my back seat. "I gave him this address, Officer. Sorry."

"Shut up, you," the officer, who was also white, demanded, and turned back to me. "I'm asking whether or not you can read," he said.

"Sorry, yes, of course I can read," I said, though I was so flustered by then that I probably would have flunked a reading test.

"Next time, it's better to be right than sorry," the police officer grumbled and stalked away.

My breathing was shallow and panicked. All I could

think of was my brother and my friend warning me to act harmless if I was driving a car and stopped by the police. "Otherwise, they might shoot you because you are a Black man."

My experiences of being Black in America, including my interactions with the police are all exasperating; since my arrival in the U.S., I have been stopped no fewer than five times by the police, several times simply for being in white neighborhoods. One police officer actually followed me simply because I had dropped a white woman off at her home in northern Massachusetts—during which I strictly adhered to the "act harmless" rule sternly laid down by my school friend.

*

The legacy of slavery in the U.S. means that Black African migrants face challenges that non-Black immigrants do not, simply due to the color of our skin. Our immigrant status means we also face challenges that U.S.-born Black Americans do not. Yet, too often, Black immigrants are missing from our conversations about what it means to be Black in the U.S. This article seeks to remedy that by raising awareness of the Black migrant experience.

In 1970, one in 100 Black Americans was an immigrant. Today, it's one out of ten, according to the Immigrant Learning Center. Africans make up the fastest-growing immigrant group in the U.S.

African migration is driven by the human desire to escape poverty, corruption, and tyranny. These circumstances are the legacy of the West's interaction with the continent: colonialism, slavery, neocolonialism, dictatorship by proxy, and corporate adventurism. That legacy is deeply enmeshed with that of nearly every country in Africa, so this article elucidates a complex picture and traces a long, historical arc.

Ours is an unprecedented time in the history of Black people in the United States. This country has a large Black population because of the transatlantic slave trade that began in the 16th century, but voluntary Black migrant workers only began arriving in the U.S. about two decades ago. Now, according to a Pew Research Center analysis, there are over 4.2 million Black immigrants living in the U.S.—a five-fold increase since 1980.

Roughly one in ten Blacks living in the U.S. today were born outside the country, and an increasingly large percentage of those Black migrants are African. Many Black Africans are so desperate to migrate to the U.S. that they have even begun coming by way of Latin America; the number of African migrants trying to cross the Mexican border has been steadily rising since 2007.

Black African migrants like me feel compelled to risk everything to leave our homelands and families for other countries—even when those countries make it abundantly clear that we are not wanted, despite the fact that we are essential to keeping the economies of those countries strong. Sometimes our journeys are risky, or even dangerous. Sometimes, they are depressing and disheartening. Whether we arrive as refugees or migrant workers, most of us suffer great losses as we become separated and fractured from our homelands, cultures, native tongues, and extended families—or even from our own children.

Meanwhile, we walk a tightrope when it comes to fitting in. At times we're praised as "hardworking immigrants" who are following in the footsteps of the immigrants who came here and made America "great," while at other times we're seen an alien invaders intent on "stealing jobs," or, worse, as terrorists and rapists.

Many of us have college degrees or even advanced degrees, while others are skilled artisans. Unfortunately, as migrants we have no choice but to take 3D (dirty, dangerous, and demeaning) jobs, working twice as hard to prove our worth not only as workers, but also as humans. We are thrust into the front lines as essential workers, especially during times like this one, when the coronavirus pandemic rages around the world. Yet, we remain invisible to both the politicians who govern our lives and the public we serve.

Despite these hardships, we will keep coming. Because there are historical, economic, and political currents that have served throughout history to carry us to Western shores, and that are still bringing us here now.

As the number of Black migrants continues to skyrocket, the Covid-19 pandemic has served to highlight the systemic racism suffered by all Blacks in the U.S. More Blacks than Whites have died or experienced long hospitalizations and severe economic losses as a result of the pandemic, largely because more Blacks Americans *and* Black migrants are working in low-paying, 3D jobs and living in substandard conditions.

*

As a Black African, I have been told "Go back to your country!" or "Go back to Africa!" many times since coming to the U.S. Sometimes by Black people like myself. For example, on my first day at work in a home for mentally disabled individuals, a Black American worker stormed into the dining coming from the office, yelling, "Why are all of you people running away from Africa and taking all of our jobs here? Go back to Africa!"

I learned that this man, Carl—who later became a friend—was apparently angry that the group manager had given me shifts that Carl had previously relied on for overtime. As I investigated further, I discovered that it was company policy to encourage managers to bring in new people to fill shifts instead of offering overtime to existing staff, since overtime would cost the company 1.5 times the hourly rate.

Carl was a single father who relied on that extra pay from overtime, so I understood his anger. Later, we explored this company policy together, and I asked, "What if the company paid you that salary ordinarily, only for your regular 40-hour work week?"

As I've delved deeper into discussions with Carl and other Black Americans I've met since coming to the U.S., I hear from many who think we are not brothers. In fact, some Black Americans I've met have preconceived notions of Africa as a continent filled with safari animals and jungles, and distance themselves from Black Africans as "lower" beings not only because we are migrants, but because they imagine we've arrived in the U.S. straight from the jungle. I discuss the Black Lives Matter movement in the context of history and my own experiences in this country.

In these discussions, I highlight the fact that some Black Americans are astonished to hear that Africans are trying to flee the Continent, since they are currently struggling against systemic racism in the U.S. and demanding reparations, and I reflect on the reparations debate currently underway in the U.S. I also tackle the news here of Africans giving up their freedom to be slaves in Libya; in late 2017, the U.S. media outlet Cable News Network (CNN) aired reports of West African migrants in the latter stages of their journey to Europe, who had been sold openly in slave markets in Libya. The reports generated widespread condemnation as audiences watched footage of Arab slave traders selling individual people—who were to be used as farm workers—for as little as $400. The CNN revelations suggested that some Africans were so desperate for freedom that they knowingly accepted the risks of entering slavery, and even American rapper Kanye West publicly speculated that the ancient practice of slavery always was predicated as a choice.

The Thorny Road to Asylum

MY meeting with my employer, the new editor-in-chief of *The National* newspaper in Abu Dhabi, lasted all of three minutes. "Your local editor has good things to say about your work, Yasin," he began. "You're known as one of the hardest working reporters." Then his expression turned grave. "Unfortunately, I have some bad news to pass along."

I had already guessed what it was, based on the fact that the government hadn't renewed my work visa. "You're firing me," I said.

He was, he admitted, because of the autobiography I'd published, *The Ambitious Struggle: An African Journalist's Journey of Hope and Identity in a Land of Migrants.*

"On what basis?" I demanded. "I wrote that book on my own time."

He looked taken aback. "Well, you never obtained clearance to get it published. And the content doesn't portray your employer in the most positive light."

"Have you read my book?" I asked.

He had not, he said.

The government had fired me, essentially, by not renewing my visa, because I'd been writing about the abuse of migrant workers and systemic racism. As a journalist in Dubai, I was following the thousands of Asian and Africans migrating to the Gulf region to make a living for their families. Unfortunately, for many the migration journey is full of deceptions, abuse, and isolation. I wanted to challenge the perception of migrant workers as commodities, both in their home and their host countries.

As one colleague told me, I should think of the termination as an honor. "Yasin," he said, "you have not been fired because of incompetence or corruption or anything bad. You are fired for raising a voice against racism, and that is a good thing."

Nonetheless, my book was banned across the UAE, and this was a professional blow. I suffered a personal blow, too, as I now faced an uncertain future and had to return to Uganda in defeat. Because the government refused to issue another visa and I was forced out of Dubai so quickly, I had to sell the UAE stocks I'd bought and my share of the internet cafe I'd invested in, all at a loss.

Back in Uganda, I found work as a public relations officer at a university some 85 miles from my home in the country, which meant I had to live in university quarters during the week. I was one of the university's highest-ranking officials, yet I brought in scarcely $200 monthly after paying the huge employment tax demanded by the Ugandan government. Unemployment levels had skyrocketed in the years I'd been away, and there was no other sort of job for a man with my background.

I didn't mind the job at the university. At least I was my own boss, spending the week trying to inspire media coverage for university events and people. What I minded was the bribery involved: In Uganda, no journalist will write a story without being bribed, since journalists make so little money and bribery is a way of life in this country under the current president.

Uganda, like most African countries, is suffering. The continent seems to be viewed as a source of natural resources that come without the burden of sustainability, and cheap labor without the cost of socio-economic responsibility or health and safety legislation. Indeed, many nations treat Africa as a dumping ground for both actual rubbish and cheaply made clothing, used electronics, or foodstuffs that were found to be in surplus or that failed to capture Western markets.

The streams of wealth leave Africa at a rate that outpaces the inflows, and how Africa's unique position in the league table of misfortune is secured by the duration and depth of her relationship with slavery and its descendant forms of exploitation. That's why so many Black African migrants flee the continent, seeking better opportunities elsewhere.

My attempt to try my hand at farming—a venture that no doubt appealed to me because, as a small boy, many of my happiest hours with my father were spent clearing land and planting sweet potatoes. I had bought a small plot of land while I was in Dubai. Now, with so little money to support my family, we moved to our unfinished country house—with no running water or electricity—and I tried my hand at farming passionfruit.

In this way, I learned the hard way what President Museveni's regime had done to Ugandan agriculture. Certainly, there were challenges from nature—for instance, it was difficult to harvest even 100 kilograms in hot weather, or when rain failed to materialize during the growing season—and when the rains did finally come, the yield was so large that prices could drop from $200 per bushel to $30. From my initial investment, I made a return of less than $5000.

Furthermore, fertilizers and pesticides, essential in any high-yield agriculture, are expensive in Uganda. They're imported from Europe and all costs are passed on to farmers, unlike in the U.S., where the costs of these things are subsidized. The availability of machinery is also an issue. I used to hire three or four people to plow my land with a hoe; they could do each acre in three days. A small tractor could have done this job in a few hours, but there were none nearby.

My children wouldn't be able to go to school if I couldn't pay for their fees, never mind the nieces and nephew living with us. My sisters, too, needed a hand to support their families, for they were making even less money than I was, despite being nurses and teachers. Soon I would have to go begging as well if money kept falling out of my pockets faster than I could refill them.

When my father died, I stood in the four-foot grave with my brothers, preparing to lower his body in the ground and concentrating on remembering the protocols of carrying the dead. I was intent on trying to handle my father's body the same way I had seen him handle others.

But I was also recalling our last conversation on his

deathbed. I grieved not only for my father, but also for the fact that I wasn't there in time to take him to the hospital when he died and couldn't pay his medical expenses in his final days. I had paid a high price to raise my voice in defense of migrants.

Still, while I had no intention of obeying my father's injunction against writing books or articles that held truth to power, I knew he was right about leaving Uganda. It was time for me to go.

Only when you lose a parent do you feel the gravity of being an adult in a complicated world.

*

Even when I arrived in America my Ugandan tormentors still haunted me. I received a call from an unknown number on WhatsApp and picked it up. Many of my relatives use this app to reach me when they're in trouble.

"Hello?" I said. "This is Yasin."

The voice on the other end was unfamiliar, male, and angry. "You think you're safe there in America," he hissed, "but I assure you that you're not."

He then proceeded to tell me the Ugandan proverb about the corn worm. This worm thinks it's safe because it hides in the ear of corn as the corn plants are being cut down, only to discover too late that it is going to be dropped into a pot of boiling water when the corn is husked.

"You are in the boiling water, Mr. Journalist," my caller announced. "You believe you can talk about anything because you're in America, but I would be very, very careful if I were you. I'd advise you to get your affairs in order because your time is coming. Be alert. You never know what will happen, or when. There are many ways to destroy a man."

I hung up, shaking, and parted the curtains of the bedroom I shared with my brother to peer outside into the chilly Boston evening.

You would think that an asylum claim would be easy to make if your life is being threatened, but you would be wrong. The road to asylum in the U.S. is potholed and dark, so that you're always feeling your way and worrying that you'll never reach the end of it.

From filing the paperwork and being interviewed to see if you deserve to be offered asylum in the U.S. is a process that's both mysterious and terrifying.

Friends asked me why I decided to apply for asylum during the Trump era, a period of hostility towards immigrants, but my attorney was convinced that my journey would be easier than most. After all, much of the evidence I presented had been published and was available online.

I compiled that material and within a few weeks my attorney assured me that I was prepared for the interview. We sought to expedite the process, hoping for a three-week turnaround, as opposed to the possible years it might take.

Several months after the interview and with no decision from the immigration authorities in sight, reality hit home and we acknowledged how wrong we had been to think that we could rush the process and that my case would be a straightforward one. In truth, there were no easy asylum cases in the U.S. Normally, the asylum process for a candidate like me would have been resolved within a few months. Now I was facing years in limbo.

The delay in the process also affected Rachel, the disabled woman I was working for as a caregiver. Almost every day she would ask me if the immigration officials had responded to my asylum interview and the answer was always no.

She was not only worried about losing a worker who could lift her up and put her in the wheelchair—a freedom she cherished—but also worried that the Trump Government might soon block all asylum applications and there would be no one to help her.

She mentioned that she could help get me a Green Card on the understanding that I wouldn't leave her after obtaining it. However, I was not certain I was willing to be her caregiver for the rest of my life.

Rachel suggested that she could contact Massachusetts U.S. Senator Edward J. Markey on my behalf and that he would be able to get me a Green Card. The process required a senator to initiate a private bill on my behalf. Such an option is extremely rare. Fewer than 100 immigrants receive such consideration annually. I told her that there was no chance, but she insisted that there was no harm in trying.

She called Markey's office and I signed papers authorizing the senator to make an inquiry regarding my case. After the inquiry, the immigration officers called my lawyer and scheduled a second interview with me.

The second interview was much shorter than the first, lasting only 20 minutes. My lawyer asked when the immigration officer expected a response and he promised it would come within three months. However, that time elapsed and the decision had not yet arrived.

*

My brother and I rarely speak on the phone, and never when we are working, so I immediately assumed the worst when he called me at Rachel's house this past February.

"What is it, Wahab? What's the matter?" I asked, my heart hammering against my rib cage. I assumed that someone we knew must have died.

"Are you bringing me to your party, Yasin?" he teased.

"What are you talking about?" I asked irritably. I had just finished changing Rachel's diaper and was in no mood for jokes.

"Congratulations, brother!" he yelled. "Your asylum is approved! I saw the letter from immigration and couldn't help myself. I opened it, and it says you've been approved. It's time for a party!"

I couldn't believe it. Three years I'd been waiting, navigating an impossible sequence of filling out papers, answering questions in interviews with government officials, and providing fingerprints and documents to prove that I could no longer live safely in Uganda.

As I quickly discovered, however, there wasn't much cause for celebration. Yes, earning asylum meant that I could now live legally in the U.S., apply for citizenship, and bring my family here. But the Ugandan government was now erecting new roadblocks, claiming that there were no birth certificates available for my children—something required for asylum seekers to bring their families to the U.S.—and, as my lawyer said, "You can expect to wait a few more years to bring them over, Yasin. It's a long process, especially with the backlog since Covid-19 shut everything down."

*

During a writer's workshop in Boston not long afterward, I had the opportunity to meet a popular Black American writer. We exchanged introductions and he said he was fascinated by my work.

"Why don't you write books or articles on similar topics?" I asked. "You're far better known than I am. You'd get more attention."

He shook his head. "There aren't any advances or grants for that sort of thing," he said. "Besides, that kind of work will never be well disseminated, because it involves criticizing the owners and managers of the very channels through which it would need to travel. So it would be useless, in the end."

I disagree. As Hemingway wrote in *For Whom the Bell Tolls*, "Defending the dignity of others is never a lost cause whether you succeed or not."

While still in Uganda I applied for the TED Fellowship Program, a global platform where expert speakers give talks that are distributed online, as my interest was more in giving a TED Talk that would put some spotlight on my activism work for the increasing numbers of African migrants being trapped, exploited, abused, and even murdered in the Gulf Arab countries. Unfortunately, by the time the TED Fellows team offered me a fellowship and a chance to give the talk I had migrated to the U.S.

I learned from an email that I had been selected. I was on my way to the library when the notification popped up on my phone. I pulled my car over to the side of the road and accepted the offer immediately, thrilled that I had been accepted. The news was a dream come true. Being selected as a TED fellow is a privilege; TED is a wonderful global platform, and I knew that, from there, ideas like mine about the universality of human rights can spread easily.

Most victims of injustices like those committed against poor migrant workers in the Middle East don't have a platform for speaking up. Now, after living in the U.S. as a Black migrant worker myself, I knew firsthand that the only difference between you and those who are abused is often simply luck.

Unfortunately, by the time the TED Fellows team offered me a fellowship and a chance to give the talk, I had migrated to the U.S. to apply for asylum. The rules for asylum seekers are strict and the process is excruciatingly slow. If you leave before asylum is granted, the application is null and void, and you can never return to the U.S.

My TED Fellowship would require me to travel to Tanzania to give my talk. I describe the agonizing decision of having to turn down this opportunity even after hiring a lawyer to help expedite the asylum interview. For a month, I was torn between working my "3 D's" immigration jobs, preparing my asylum papers with the lawyer to help expedite the process, and writing the TED Talk that I realized I might never deliver.

When I finally told the TED team about the travel restrictions, they promised to put me back on the roster of future TED Talks once my asylum process was concluded, and in December 2017 my name appeared again on another list for the April 2018 TED Talks. I panicked and tried to fast-track everything to be able to travel to Vancouver and speak. I had completed my asylum interview in September 2017 and expected a decision any time, but it had yet to arrive. Around the end of January 2018, I gave up and asked the TED Team to allow me to give my talk virtually.

When I arrived in New York to tape my TED talk in their offices, it was surreal to suddenly be seen as who I really am an academic, scholar, and activist, instead of a caregiver strong enough to lift someone out of bed and into a wheelchair. I was offered coffee and lunch, and asked if I was comfortable. The theme of my talk was "Why Africans Are Migrating to Europe, the Middle East and the USA." I watched it on my laptop livestream during the conference. It gained a record million views within the first month of being aired and it is still available online. I was excited and I deeply appreciated the TED Talks team for its efforts and for recognizing the significance, breadth and depth of this issue of why African migrants search so desperately for their own economic reward and for justice.

Conclusion and Call to Action

IN the November 2018 elections there was a proposed ballot question in Massachusetts to mandate nurse staffing ratios in hospitals, depending upon a specific unit of services, and the bill pitted health care employers against nurses.

The Massachusetts Nurses Association that initiated the bill argued that safe staffing ratios are necessary to ensure that nurses are able to care adequately for patients. They relied on reports from registered nurses who are assigned an excessive caseload of patients to care for within a single time, which can result in medication errors, longer hospital stays, or accidental patient injury. They cited studies that show higher rates of complications when nurses are caring for more patients than what can be managed satisfactorily.

However, the Massachusetts Health and Hospital Association opposed the bill and spent millions in ads, urging people to vote against the initiative. The group also commissioned a study, which found that mandating nurse staffing ratios would cost the Massachusetts health care system $1.3 billion in the first year and $900 million each year after that.

The initiative failed at the polls, with 70 percent of voters rejecting it but the campaign also managed to push the question of the understaffed and overburdened nurses to the public's view.

A critical component of this debate that was entirely absent from public discourse concerned immigrants. The nursing profession employs many migrants, but with current restrictions there are growing concerns about leaving that demand unmet. While employers and hospitals fought successfully against this particular initiative, the problem of staffing is likely to worsen.

Politicians have convinced citizens in their respective countries that migrants are a competitive threat to their jobs. This virulently nativist message has been driven through mainstream media without addressing the question of whether experts in labor economics have found evidence to support or challenge this position.

Politicians rushing to portray themselves as champions of worker's rights have proposed anti-immigrant policies as protectionist measures of citizens workers without considering if, indeed, the policy makes economic sense.

This deception is widespread and has been difficult to shake free of, but the real context of the debate is one that few people care to consider publicly.

Take for example the *types* of jobs many migrants take in the U.S. Even people with advanced degrees (such as me), or those who have trained as doctors and lawyers have felt compelled to take jobs that are far beneath their education and experience. And, these are jobs that certainly no American with comparable training would dream to take. Few people seem to wonder why highly educated and professionally trained migrants are passed over for jobs that require such skills and instead are directed toward lower-paying menial jobs that have traditionally been difficult to fill.

Here is a position that rarely enters the public debate: American-born and migrant workers have common concerns about employers who exploit them. Rather than frame the discussion in an adversarial perspective, it would be wise to consider the labor rights issue from the overlapping concerns of both groups of workers.

Politicians consciously deploy rhetoric to manipulate lower-income and lower-middle class groups into blaming angry migrant workers for their troubles. It is a distractive ploy that undermines the pervasive and genuine concerns that American workers have held for a long time as they have seen their labor rights diminish while corporate protections have led to record-setting profits and wages have stagnated, even during strong periods of economic recovery and growth (as in the case of the U.S. economy as it rebounded from the Great Recession of 2008).

Antagonism from native workers towards immigrants is nothing new of course. Writing in *Black Marxism; The Making of the Black Radical Tradition*, Cedric J. Robinson notes that in the early 20th century in the U.S., black and non-black workers opposed each other. The northern non-black working-class movement effectively excluded the freedmen, the slaves, and the five million poor whites of the south.

Today, in the U.S., many customer service companies have outsourced work to India, South Africa, the Philippines, and elsewhere. The incentive to pay lower wages is strong. For example, an entry-level IT worker in China might be paid $7,000 a year and $8,400 in India.

U.S. employers have chosen to locate their call centers in India and the Philippines because residents in those countries speak English. Every time Rachel my personal care assistants' boss has called Amazon, she has asked the person who answered the call where they are based. She enjoys mocking their countries and often teases them about their heavily accented English, especially if they are from India or South Africa.

Meanwhile, few Americans consider that many corporate enterprises also are buying millions of acres of land parcels in Africa, which displace homeland natives and turns them into migrants seeking labor abroad. Rarely, anyone traces the entire cycle of what is happening while leaving politicians' remarks about the issue unchallenged.

To reiterate, many migrants do jobs that many American citizens will not take. When I worked for nearly a year in residential group homes for persons with developmental disabilities, I did not encounter a single American citizen, especially in overnight shifts.

It is hard to make the case that migrants have made a negative impact on the job picture in the States. In fact, citizens might view immigrants in a more complimentary way because with their coming to take care of their relatives such as elderly parents or loved ones with developmental disabilities they free up the time of citizens to pursue their career and professional paths more effectively.

If the mother of a child with developmental disabilities she had to keep the child at home, stay awake all night and monitor all day, she would not have time to work in an office or to pursue education or professional advancement. Again, few people connect the dots in the network chain that facilitates these opportunities.

The example of immigrants taking up jobs for elderly care in the U.S.—positions that few American-born citizens have been willing to fill—not only satisfies in part a strong employment demand but also has helped to keep unemployment low. But, more importantly, immigrants also have helped to solve in part an imminent and potentially far-reaching social crisis, taking care of elderly citizens, who are frail and/ or no longer have the mental capacities to care for themselves. So much is discussed about the quality of health care in the country without ever considering the essential role that so many migrant workers at the front line of such service are filling without the benefit of exaggerated wages or costs.

Immigration also has an economic impact that has managed to keep inflation in check even with low unemployment rates. In the early years of the 21ˢᵗ century, the large pool of low-skill immigrant workers, especially from Mexico, who came to California made it cheaper for citizens to have their houses cleaned and lawns mowed. Likewise, the demand for workers on farms to pick and process local produce was substantial.

But, while politicians have argued for anti-immigrant policies, the nature of migration has changed dramatically, effectively making the political messages moot and irrelevant. By 2016, the number of immigrants coming to California from Mexico, according to the Public Policy Institute of California, has declined significantly by more than 70 percent since 2000. This means that fewer than 150,000 Mexican citizens now come annually to California.

Indeed, California now received more migrants from China than it does from Mexico and, if current trends continue, then India, the Philippines, and Vietnam will all soon be above Mexico in that league table. Many of California's newer immigrants have much higher education levels, including a completed baccalaureate degree according to the Institute:

"The sharp increase in highly educated immigrants and the decline in less-educated immigrants reflect the changing labor market in California. Unemployment rates for workers with at least a bachelor's degree (3.3 percent) are about half those of less-educated workers (6.5 percent). With California expected to face a shortfall of 1.1 million college graduates by 2030, highly educated immigrants are a key component to helping the

state address the workforce skills gap."

Migrants are essential to keeping the U.S. economy competitive in rapidly evolving global markets, as they open firms, adopt innovative market practices, and create additional jobs. More than 40 percent of all Fortune 500 companies in U.S. were founded by immigrants. Three-quarters of patents from top universities in 2011 had a foreign-born inventor.

In addition, immigrants account for a large share of Nobel Prizes: 33 percent in chemistry, 26 percent in economics, 34 percent in medicine, for example. While current U.S. politicians insist on short-sighted critiques of immigrant labor without considering the ramifications of changing a system that has not been revamped since 1965, a time when both the American and global economies were so different from their current renditions.

At some point, the migration crisis will become an existential one for human civilization. The solution to it should be human based on the principle that everyone—regardless of their country of origin—should be treated fairly. It seems simple but hitherto has proved politically elusive, but it remains possible.

END

Coming Soon

A MURDER OF HATE
The General's Project Book series 1 of 3

When Boston detectives Lisa Garcia and Basudde "Bus" Erias are enlisted to solve the brutal murder of an African president's exchange-student niece, the two rival investigators unravel not only the identity of the killer, but also expose deadly ties between Washington elites and the dictators they support.

Coming Soon

THE MISSING CORPSE
The General's Project Book series 2 of 3

When CIA intelligence catches wind of a shocking revelation—a general and son of an African president suspected of murdering his father and concealing the body until he seizes power—they send in their top agent, Shawn Wayles, to gather crucial intelligence. Teaming up with an LGBTQ couple, Shawn embarks on a daring mission to retrieve the president's body from the clutches of the GENERAL'S security team. As the general scrambles to recover the missing corpse, a high-stakes game ensues, where possession of the body equates to ultimate power.